REDISCOVERING THE MINISTRY OF BLESSING

REDISCOVERING THE MINISTRY OF BLESSING

Russ Parker

SPCK

First published in Great Britain in 2014

Society for Promoting Christian Knowledge
36 Causton Street
London SW1P 4ST
www.spckpublishing.co.uk

British Library Cataloguing-in-Publication Data
A catalogue record for this book is available from the British Library

ISBN 978–0–281–06981–1
eBook ISBN 978–0–281–06982–8

Typeset by Graphicraft Limited, Hong Kong
First printed in Great Britain by Ashford Colour Press
Subsequently digitally printed in Great Britain

eBook by Graphicraft Limited, Hong Kong

Produced on paper from sustainable forests

I dedicate this book to the amazing staff and volunteers of the Acorn Christian Healing Foundation with whom I have served for 24 years. Thank you so much for your tremendous devotion to the ministry of listening, healing and reconciliation. It has been a joy and also lots of fun and hard work.

Contents

Introduction

Some years ago I was the keynote speaker at a conference for Roman Catholic prayer leaders in Italy and was launching my book, *Forgiveness Is Healing*, at the same time. When I arrived I discovered it had, without my knowledge, been published in Italian and that this version was selling remarkably well whereas my own, official, version remained unsold. Needless to say I was very concerned and upset. Then in the middle of all this a woman came up to me and not only asked me to sign her copy of the offending book but also to pray for her! I did my best to swallow my pride, signed her book and then laid hands on her head and prayed (without being translated), 'Lord! Give this woman the biggest blessing she can live with.' She immediately rested in the Spirit and later told me that she had experienced an overwhelming sense of God's special love for her. She said that it lifted the heaviness that she had grown accustomed to living with and believed from this that her lifelong battle with depression was at last being won. She believed that she was healed.

Following this blessing prayer, in a matter of moments I had a queue of people clamouring for prayer ministry. As I could not speak Italian I prayed the same prayer over them all in rapid succession. So many of them rested in the Spirit as the touch of God came on their lives. Such was the demand for prayer that the rest of the conference was given over to this and I never did give the rest of my scheduled talks. I don't mind admitting that I felt out of my depth and awed at the presence of God to heal so powerfully. I was even assigned a couple of 'minders' who would make sure I had some space to myself. During the course of that day many people reported to Father Di Fulvio, the convenor of the conference, that God had healed them of their sicknesses. Among the range of stunning healings reported were those from deafness, sight impairment, physical pain and terminal cancer. It took my breath away, and when I sat down with God after three days of almost non-stop praying in this way and reflected on what had happened, the Lord showed me that this was the power of blessing.

Thus began for me an adventure of discovering the lost ministry of blessing. Up to this point the word 'blessing' had been for me a reference to praying for God to answer my prayers and do something good in someone's life. There were no specifics attached to praying, 'Lord, bless this person; Lord, bless our church.' It was Christian shorthand asking God to do something or to bring well-being. Not a bad thing to desire of course, but if we are honest with ourselves this kind of praying carries with it the hazard of becoming boring after a while, with an almost zero level of expectation.

It is this carte-blanche use of the term that we find the world over. When someone sneezes we say, 'Bless you!' When a baby does something endearing we say, 'Oh, how sweet. Bless!' And there is still to be found the odd prospective son-in-law who will ask the father of his intended bride if he can have his consent, or blessing, to marry his daughter. They all convey the wish to see good fortune for someone. Yet as we shall see later in this book, the Bible teaches us that blessing is a unique ministry resource gifted to believers to effect the purposes of God in people's lives. And like any other ministry procedure, it has its own rules and rhythms of grace.

My exploration of the ministry of blessing was greatly helped when I read *The Grace Outpouring* by Roy Godwin and Dave Roberts.[1] It is a collection of marvellous stories spread over a number of years in which the giving of blessing transformed many lives and brought some people to a living faith in Jesus Christ. Roy and his wife Daphne became the resident directors of a Christian retreat centre named Ffald-y-Brenin ('Sheepfold of the king'), which is situated in the Berwyn mountains not far from Fishguard in South Wales. Roy confesses that he was feeling rather unfulfilled in this role as his passion was for evangelism and he could not really see how he could fulfil this ministry in a quiet and remote part of Wales. He set himself to prayer. The breakthrough came when a couple arrived at the retreat centre not really knowing what it was all about. In fact the husband reported that he felt compelled to visit the place and so drove up the driveway. Roy showed them around, gave them the tour. Finally he took them to the newly completed chapel and rather than witness to the couple in his time-honoured fashion he felt led to pray a prayer of blessing over them. He told them, 'We have a new rule here about how to respond to our visitors. We like to bless them before they leave. May I bless you?'[2] The actual prayer prayed was, 'I bless you in the name of Jesus to know God, his purpose for your life, and his blessings on you and your family and the situations of your life. Amen.' It was then that they started to weep, and Roy left them so that they could have time to themselves. They later shared how they felt profoundly moved by being in the chapel and by how the gospel of Christ was shared with them. It seems that that prayer of blessing had set them on a road of awakening to the love of God.

That simple prayer blessing became the hallmark of the ministry at Ffald-y-Brenin as this couple were followed by a stream of visitors with the same sense of compulsion to visit the site where so many strangers found the love and saving power of God in their lives. Since then this retreat centre has drawn people from all over the world, who on coming to it find a new and living relationship with Jesus Christ. It is a modern-day site of holy pilgrimage to which people have been drawn from all over the world seeking the touch of God upon their lives in a new and deeper way. Some have experienced physical healing, others have found fresh encounters with the love of God that has restored hope and purpose to their Christian walk of faith.

I have introduced this subject by telling you some stories, but read on: I will back this up by looking at the wealth of material in the Scriptures about this unique ministry of blessing, and it is my hope that you will as a result become someone who practises this ministry to equal effect in your own life and work.

1

Words of blessing

> The first thing that God did after He created man in His own image was to bless him![1]

The term 'blessing' has travelled a long distance in its meaning and usage over the last two millennia. It literally began in blood. The word is traced back to the eighth-century Old Teutonic German *bletsian*, which referred to blood sacrifices and is closely related to the word *blōd*, which means 'blood'. The *Shorter Oxford English Dictionary* suggests that it refers to something – an animal for sacrifice – or someone marked with blood prior to being offered in sacrificial ritual. The term then emerges in Old English of the tenth century as *blaedsian*. The modern meaning may have been influenced in translations of the Bible into Old English during the process of Christianizing in Western Europe, where it was used to translate the Latin *benedicere* and its Greek counterpart *eulogeitos*, meaning 'to speak well of'. As a result the word began to be used to express meanings such as to praise, extol or wish well. You can be forgiven for thinking that we have tamed or 'dumbed down' its original impact or meaning.

Reflecting for a moment on this brief etymological study, we can see that embedded in the word is a sense of costliness and gratitude and holiness. To be blessed will involve the shedding of blood and for Christians this immediately takes us to Calvary and the blessing of the gift of salvation that is ours to receive because another has made possible what we could not achieve by ourselves. There is always that sense in which we are indebted to the one who underwent sacrifice for the benefits it affords us. We are literally marked by those benefits, whether they be forgiveness, guidance or healing. It would not be out of place to say that such sacrificial blessings are an impartation of holiness or the touch of God on our lives. It is tangible and intended to be transformational, for all such sacrifices invite us to walk in the newness of life that is the very heart of our Christian gospel. As we shall see later, whether by blood sacrifice or via spoken words, the blessing is intended to have impact and to leave us with the imprint of God's touch and benefits on our lives.

The Old Testament and blessings on bended knee

The Hebrew words for blessing in the Old Testament are *barakh* and *berakhah*, and they are both derived from a word that means 'knee'. They are used over 400 times in the Scriptures, and rarely refer to the physical act of kneeling. At their core the terms mean to show respect, and this is often accompanied by bowing or bending the knee. A good question to ask at this point is, 'Who is bowing the knee? Is it the one being blessed or the one offering the blessing?' The obvious answer perhaps is that it is the one receiving the blessing who has knelt down in humility to receive from the other. However, entertain for the moment the concept of God bowing the knee. I do not mean that God is subject to his creation, but it does display quite graphically the servant heart of God who longs to meet the needs of his broken world. This is more than echoed in the actions of Jesus, who summarized his whole ministry in terms of the Lord who comes to serve (Luke 22.27). The great hymn of Philippians paints a similar picture of the incarnate God coming in the form of a servant (Phil. 2.7). It is humbling to think of God honouring in such fashion, and as such it describes for us our heart's attitude when we bless others: we wish to serve the best interests of others that they may grow and flourish as God wills for them.

The *Theological Wordbook of the Old Testament* states that 'to bless means to endue with power for success, prosperity, fecundity and longevity'.[2] This picks up the issue of impartation once again. The blessing received does not consist merely of nice words and hopeful aspirations but brings with it the expectation that God is changing things in our lives, which is evident by the differences made in those lives.

One of the first examples of this in Scripture occurs in Genesis 12.2, where God says to Abram, 'I will bless you; I will make your name great.' The patriarch is being encouraged to step out of his comfort zone into an adventure with God in a new country, and although he would begin with little or nothing in terms of worldly wealth and influence, the nature of the blessing God would eventually give him would be to make him a man of substance and influence beyond his imagination. We must not mistake this for a prosperity gospel but a promise from God that he would put his mark on this man if he kept true to his divine guidance, and would transform him to be someone whom others recognized as favoured by God. His greatness would not lie in his possessions but in his being possessed by God.

This in fact became the hallmark of the covenants that God made with Abraham and his descendants and community. God promised not only to bless Abraham and his descendent community but also to make them a blessing to the nations (Gen. 12.2–3). This blessing is not to be kept but to be shared and given away; it is to be imparted to others. The identity or shape of the blessings to be visited on the nations are not specified but the implication is that they will have prosperity and security under the protection of God. The covenant blessing is repeated in Genesis 17 and is extended to the barren Sarah, to whom it would come in the form of pregnancy and motherhood of a longed-for son (v. 16). The blessing of security for a future is even extended to Ishmael (v. 20). Isaac is encouraged to settle temporarily on the foreign soil of Gerar but is helped through the process with the promise from God that if he does this he will be blessed so that someday he would cease to be an alien in the land and become its owner (Gen. 3—4; 26.1–6). Jacob in his battling with the angel of the Lord suddenly cried out in desperation, 'I will not let you go unless you bless me' (Gen. 32.26). It seems he was convinced that he was about to be abandoned by God himself, hence his 'de profundis' or cry from the depths of his soul. We are told that after confessing his name of Jacob, God changes his identity to Israel, and this becomes the foundation on which God blesses him there and then. Although he hobbled away into his future, his blessing was already carrying him to the destiny of becoming a father of nations.

Blessings and curses

However, these blessings are to be given and experienced within the keeping of the covenant loyalty to Yahweh. So we need to acknowledge that blessings can also be lost. Much later Moses reminds the newly emerging community called Israel of their covenant heritage and presents God's challenge to them:

> I am setting before you today a blessing and a curse – the blessing if you obey the commands of the Lord your God that I am giving you today; the curse if you disobey . . . and turn from the way . . . by following other gods. (Deuteronomy 11.26–28)

Blessing and cursing are close experiences on this basis because they are both related to the consequences of observing the covenant of God or not. It does present a strong argument that blessings and curses are not neutral experiences that can be taken or left according to our choices but are the expected outcomes of faithfulness or rebellion. Just as blessing signifies something that God adds to our lives so the word curse, its opposite, signifies that destructive and corrosive power that means to take away from or to be diminished and blemished. This parallel of covenant-keeping versus covenant-breaking comes to full explanation in some of the final teaching Moses gave the community of Israel as they prepared to enter the promised land. Blessing is the reward and fruit of faithfulness and being cursed is the fruit of disobedience. There is a long list of the misdemeanours and then the curse content is identified and consists of loss of health, both for people and places. There will be total frustration in their attempts to farm the land and build safe community and the ultimate effect is the loss of ownership of the land and destruction of the community itself (Deut. 28.20–46). A graphic illustration of this parallel power of blessings and cursing is found in the example of the professional seer Balaam. He is hired by Balak, the Canaanite monarch of Moab, to curse the tribes of Israel as he is afraid they will conquer his lands (Num. 22.1–6). Interestingly enough, Balak acknowledges that this prophet's curses and blessings have the power to deliver precisely their intended outcome (Num. 22.6). The story is told in great detail of how the seer sets out to accomplish what he has been paid to do, but runs into the God of Israel who commands him to bless and not to curse. Needless to say this greatly angers Balak, who continually confronts the prophet to finish the job he has been paid to do. Balaam's final response is to inform the king of Moab, 'I could not do anything of my own accord, good or bad, to go beyond the command of the Lord' (Num. 24.13). Here is an insight to this developing understanding of blessing, that it must cohere with the known will and purposes of God. Blessings are a declaration of the will of God and have no currency or effect if divorced from that truth.

However we understand passages like this and their application to all societies and locations, or whether we limit them to Old Testament covenant community, they nonetheless teach us that blessings and curses are some form of power encounter. The words of blessing are expected to lead to advantageous changes in lives and curses are expected to take away from us that which promotes life, health and peace. Blessings and curses are effective because they are carried forward in their impact by the power and purposes of God. This needs to be especially borne in mind when we look at examples of people blessing people.

The right to bless

We have established that it is God who blesses us and especially those who stay faithful to their covenant identity. Yet it is also clear that people declared blessings on others too. Before he died Moses declared a blessing prophecy on all of the 12 tribes of Israel (Deut. 33). I describe these blessings as prophecy because they largely consist of a mixture of a character reference, a hope for the future and a judgement on their enemies. Take for example the tribe of Levi, which is praised for faithfully channelling the word of God to its community and keeping the worship structures of God alive and vital. Moses pronounced on them, 'Bless, O Lord, his substance, and accept the work of his hands; crush the loins of his adversaries, of those that hate him, so that they do not rise again' (Deut. 33.11–12 NRSV). It is clear that Moses pronounces this blessing but he acknowledges that the power to enact the effect of the wanted blessing is God's alone. Later we will explore further this effective link between spoken blessings and expected outcomes, and the relationship of faith in God and the authority to act in this way.

A prime example of people blessing people in the Old Testament is the subject of inheritance, when fathers were expected to pass on their blessings or substance to their sons. So Isaac blesses both Jacob and Esau and Jacob later repeats the same apparent mistake of preferring the younger over the older brother when he blesses Joseph's sons (Gen. 48.14–20). Joseph confronts his elderly father and thinks to correct him from his mistake, but Jacob is insistent that it is not a mistake; his blessing is the announcing of prophetic destiny on the two boys. Once again this underlines that at the core of blessing is the power of God to affect our status and destiny. We are well beyond wishful thinking and hope and into speaking with authority.

In the New Testament Jesus encourages us to bless those who curse us. 'Bless those who curse you, pray for those who mistreat you' (Luke 6.28). The apostle Paul repeats this exhortation in his letter to the Romans (Rom. 12.14; cf. 1 Cor. 4.12). As we shall see, this injunction is not just a remedy for resisting the temptation to give in to hostility towards those who persecute us but is a reflection on a larger commission to be the people who have a God-given command to bless others as a ministry of faith.

The New Testament blessings and words of powerful speech

There are two major words in the New Testament that we translate as blessing. One is to do with the powerful effects of consecrated speech, the other describes the condition or status of those who are blessed.

The first word is *eulogia*, which sounds very similar to our English word 'eulogy'. I once came across a rather cynical definition of eulogy as 'the lies we tell about people at their funerals'! It is amazing how people suddenly become paragons of virtue once they have died. I remember attending the funeral service of my great-aunt Rosie in Beckenham Crematorium in South London.

The minister who conducted her funeral had never met Rosie and he had telephoned some of her sons for information about her. In his eulogy he began to describe a woman I had never met. Apparently she was an inspiration to virtue for all who knew her and was the gentlest of souls. As he described her in these superlatives my mind drifted away to a time I unexpectedly visited her with my daughter Emma, who was about four years old at the time. Rosie was obviously somewhat nervous when we called but nonetheless eventually let us into her highrise apartment. As we talked and caught up on each other's news my daughter went exploring around the flat and came back to me quite quickly. She was a little excited and whispered into my ear, 'Dad, there's a man hiding in the wardrobe.' I was stunned to hear this and wondered what on earth she was talking about. Rosie then came clean and said that we had discovered her secret, which was that she was living with another man who was not her husband. Now I should point out that my great-aunt Rosie was a widow and was well into her eighties at this time! Arthur, the man in question, was a similar age, and had managed to smuggle himself into a large wardrobe along with his Zimmer frame.

Their relationship, by the way, was one of companionship and care, and I doubt, considering their poor health and age, that it consisted of anything more. As I remembered this story I realized that it bore no resemblance to the one being painted by the minister, and frankly I felt cheated of her story at this funeral. I loved my Aunt Rosie. I do not necessarily condone her lifestyle, which also included a hefty alcohol regime, but the eulogy was mere flattery and did not touch any of us where we needed to be that day.

So this word is not the giving of flattery or well-meaning platitudes. It basically means to 'speak well of' or 'praise'. Yet we must not confuse this with the concept of wishing people well or good fortune – it is much more specific in intent than this. This is the word that is used over 400 times in the Greek Bible, the Septuagint, to translate the word *barak*. Many of these references to praise are addressed to God in recognition of his goodness to us and our desire to give him due glory and recognition. Zechariah, the father of the newly born John the Baptist, gives praise to God when his speech is restored (Luke 1.64); Simeon praises God when he cradles the infant Jesus in his arms because he has been allowed to live long enough to see the Messiah (Luke 2.28); and James, in his pragmatic manner, reminds us that our tongues can be used equally either to bless God or curse those made in his image (James 3.9).

It is this same word that is used to describe the act of blessing others. We have already mentioned the command from Jesus to bless those who persecute us (Luke 6.28). This command is repeated enough times in the New Testament to alert us to its significance and power for our own well-being when under fire from our enemies. We will explore this in more detail later, but let me illustrate one example of this that encouraged me.

I was attending a conference on reconciliation in Singapore, and one of the contributors was an emaciated pastor called Ffon who had suffered greatly for his faith during the Vietnamese conflict. He had been brought to the conference from his home in Cambodia, and as he sat in his chair he was so small that his feet hardly touched the ground. He told his story of living on the infamous Ho Chi Minh trail through which arms were smuggled into North Vietnam. The

United States Air Force had dropped toxic canisters of so-called 'agent orange' along this trail, with the aim of despoiling the countryside and its protective foliage so that troop movements could be better targeted. The toxins contained in those canisters caused widespread sickness and death among the people who lived there.

It was in this context that Ffon lived and came to a living faith in Jesus Christ. He became a successful evangelist and church planter, and because of this came to the attention of the communist military operating in his country. He was imprisoned and chained to a stake for some considerable time, the effects of which were all too evident that day in Singapore.

However, as he was speaking he was interrupted by a man who came forward and knelt at his feet and who informed him that he was indeed the military commander responsible for his imprisonment. Apparently it was Ffon's witness that had largely contributed to his own conversion. He shared how during the times when he persecuted Ffon, the prisoner continually responded by blessing him with statements that God so loved him and the Vietnamese nation. What happened next was a holy moment for me.

The little man on the chair reached down his hands to the person kneeling at his feet and began blessing him and saying he blessed the Vietnamese people for the love they had for their country. He found every positive reason he could for pronouncing God's blessing on this man. I had a powerful glimpse of Jesus, the wounded healer, pouring his grace through the emaciated man to touch the penitent at his feet, and the guilt of the years rolled off this man and he rose to his feet positively glowing. I saw the power of blessing once again.

Jesus is of course the principal 'blesser' in the New Testament. In the first sermon of the apostle Peter he summarizes the ministry of the resurrected Jesus as the one whom God sent first to the Jews to bless them by turning them away from their 'wicked ways' (Acts 3.26). So the tangible evidence of the nation being blessed is salvation, that its people enter into holiness of life in Christ. As we look at the life and ministry of Jesus we see that woven through it are moments when he blesses bread and thousands are fed (Mark 6.41), and raises the importance of children by laying his hands on them and blessing them (Mark 10.15–16). At his last supper with his friends he describes this first communion as a cup of blessing (1 Cor. 10.16) and challenges a whole city to redeem its story by exhorting it to be the community that can say with faith, 'Blessed is the one who comes in the name of the Lord' (Matt. 23.39 NRSV).

It is this proactive ministry of blessing that Christians are to take up and pass on in their witness to and care of others. When Paul was writing to the Christians in Rome and mentioned his intention to visit them and others in Spain en route, he described his forthcoming ministry to be one where he will come 'In the fullness of the blessing of Christ' (Rom. 15.28–29 NRSV). This is not only a reference to sharing all the benefits of salvation that he has experienced but to being a blessing to others, and this will at some times include the act of pronouncing blessing on them.

The second Greek word for blessing is *makarios*. It is the one used for the Beatitudes mentioned in the Gospels of Matthew and Luke, where Jesus describes the expected status of those who are blessed. This concept of declaring a person blessed is familiar to us from the Old Testament and has the punchline of how God can reverse for the better the values by which we live. It is the poor, the meek, the faithful and the persecuted who receive the blessings of God. The term is used exclusively for people except for the two occasions where it describes God (1 Tim. 1.11; 6.15). The word is translated as 'happy' but we must not equate this simply with the feelgood factor. It is not the equivalent of the old Scouting motto of 'A Scout smiles and whistles under all difficulties', but refers more to the status God confers on those who put their trust in him. 'In the New Testament it refers overwhelmingly to the distinctive religious joy which accrues to a man from his share in the salvation of the kingdom of God.'[3] At the heart of the joy of the blessed is the tangible substance of God's touch on their lives for time and eternity. This is what Paul is underlining when he writes to the Ephesian church and says, 'Blessed be the God and Father of our Lord Jesus Christ, who has blessed us in Christ with every spiritual blessing in the heavenly places' (Eph. 1.3 NRSV). He then goes on to list the catalogue of mighty things that God has done through Jesus for our salvation and the destiny of wholeness and holiness that lies before us.

The New Testament has quite a list of those who are declared blessed. We will look at the Beatitudes in a separate chapter, but this list includes Mary the mother of Jesus, who is declared blessed more because of her faith than the fact that she carried the child of promise (Luke 1.45, 48). The disciples are blessed when they use their eyes and ears to understand parables (Matt. 13.16; Luke 10.23). Jesus declares blessed those future Christians who will believe in him without seeing him (John 20.29). Paul describes as blessed those who receive the good news by faith and not works (Rom. 4.6–9; 14.22), and James begins and ends with declaring blessed those who endure faithfully the trials of life (James 1.12; 5.11).

All of these declarations contain not only a hope for the future but an expected realization of what it means to be blessed. Consequently these are not just statements of hope but also of intent.

In summarizing our exploration of blessing in the Bible we can see that a blessing is not so much a prayer of aspiration, intercession and hope but a pronouncement of expectation on others. If there is no following through of stating the words in the anticipated shape or content of that blessing, it is not a blessing. Second, it is given to the people of faith to make such pronouncements on others. Our model in the Scriptures is God himself and as such it is characterized in the ministry of Jesus. And as Christian disciples we need to take this aspect of the power of Christ to heart and rediscover our ministry of blessing. Be the people that bless!

2

Blessings begin at home

> When you have eaten and are satisfied, you shall bless the LORD your God for the good land which He has given you.
>
> (Deuteronomy 8.10 NASB)

I can remember clearly the very first meal I ever had in a Christian home. It was in the home of the Green family in Quorn in Leicestershire. I was their guest as I was part of a Faith Mission team billeted in their village. On the wall was the very familiar quote of 'Christ is the unseen guest at every meal, the silent listener to every conversation.' The family not only gave thanks for the food that had been prepared but when the meal was over they once again gave thanks for the blessings that a good meal had given them and looked to God to take the good done to them by the meal as a reminder that they too were to leave the table and do good to someone else. It was my first experience of linking something as basic as steak and kidney pie and three vegetables with the ministry to reach out to others with the good news of the kingdom of God. I have never forgotten the lesson. Thankfulness and mission should never be separated.

This vital connection is enshrined in the commands of God in the Old Testament, especially in the book of Deuteronomy. The newly emerging nation of Israel was poised to enter the land of promise after 430 years of captivity in Egypt, and before crossing the River Jordan they were given commands and principles by which they would successfully occupy and prosper in the land. They were commanded to make sure that when they ate their meals and were satisfied, they blessed God for providing their needs and so respected the land in which they would live.

There is an awesome promise given through Moses as they were poised to cross the Sinai desert. This verse links holiness with health and blessing:

> Do not bow down before their [Canaanite] gods or worship them or follow their practices . . . Worship the LORD your God, and his blessing will be on your food and water. I will take away sickness from among you, and none will miscarry or be barren in your land. I will give you a full life span.
>
> (Exodus 23.24–26)

This is the first time in Scripture this link is made between faithfulness and blessings. Yet it becomes the template for the development of this theme throughout the Old Testament covenant with Israel. It is developed into a prophetical and liturgical act when the tribes of Israel arrive in the land promised to them. They were to form two groups of tribes, which were commanded to stand opposite each other on the mountain tops of Gerizim and Ebal. One group was to pronounce the curses that would befall them if they disobeyed God's holy commands, the other were to pronounce blessings that come from living a life of obedience (Deut. 11.26–32). In their commentary on the Old Testament, Keil and Delitzsch say that these two mountains were chosen because they stood in the very centre of the promised land, not only from west to east but also from north to south.[1] Some commentators believe that the blessings were assigned to Mount Gerizim because it had a fertile ravine on one side while Ebal was completely barren. Another reason for choosing these mountains was that being in the centre of the promised land they would ever after serve as a silent witness to the covenant made between God and the emerging nation of Israel.[2]

Elsewhere in the book of Deuteronomy these curses and blessings are listed in detail.[3] Yet when we take a close look at the blessings we see that their focus is almost exclusively domestic – they were to promote wholeness and harmony in the home and community:

> GOD's blessing inside the city,
> GOD's blessing in the country;
> GOD's blessing on your basket and bread bowl;
> GOD's blessing on your children,
> the crops of your land,
> the young of your livestock,
> the calves of your herds,
> the lambs of your flocks.

> God's blessing in your coming in,
> God's blessing in your going out.
>
> (Deuteronomy 28.3–6 *The Message*)

Consequently we can see that the Old Testament covenant enshrined the connections between faithfulness to God and the blessings that would result, namely well-being in the home and the community. We should note that the blessings are given by God, but this gave rise within the subsequent Jewish tradition of the practice of pronouncing blessings over a whole range of domestic circumstances. As we shall see, these blessing prayers or *berakhot* prayers linked the sovereignty of God in action to the activity of prayer. They were a witness and an expectation that the Lord would be touching their lives as their prayers touched the event in question. We shall now explore the links between *berakhot* prayers, the prayers of blessing from Jesus and the current revival of interest in this kind of prayer through the witness of the Celtic Christians.

However, before we do this we must ask ourselves the question of whether the Old Testament covenant has any relevance for the Christian today or whether it is exclusively for the nation of Israel. We do need to acknowledge the unique application of this covenant to Israel and at the same time emphasize that the principles and lessons enshrined in them are to be applied to all people of the Judeo–Christian faith.

The berakhot *prayers*

These are prayed as part of the normal synagogue worship and as a response or prerequisite to a wide variety of daily occurrences. All *berakhot* prayers are instantly recognizable as they begin with the sentence, 'Blessed art thou, Lord our God, King of the universe.' Many of these prayers were composed by Ezra and his associates nearly 2,500 years ago. It is worth knowing that they were born and forged in the context of return from exile and the reforming of the faithful community. The word 'thou' may sound rather formal and old-fashioned to our ears today, but in Hebrew (*atah*) it is informal and is the word used for friends and relatives. So these prayers begin with reflecting an intimacy with God. Then the body of the prayer shifts to the third person, such as 'Blessed are You, Lord our God, King of the universe, Who has sanctified us with His commandments and commands us' (Prayer of Commandment). This is intentional as it combines both the immediacy and intimacy of God as well as the sovereignty and transcendence of God.

Berakhot prayers are addressed to God as they put the emphasis on the fact that it is God who blesses and who is the power behind all our blessings of others. These prayers are riddled with expectation. They are the anticipations that God will indeed act with and through these prayers of blessing to produce the outcome enshrined in the prayer. As Kittel remarks:

> According to this belief something material comes with the blessing. Once set in motion, as when a father blesses his child, the operation is irresistible unless thwarted by equally strong opposing forces. Men and things which are blessed are as it were endowed with this power and can transmit it, affecting everything with which they come in contact. What has been said applies to the fullest possible degree when the blessing comes directly from the deity. In this case it is a 'supernatural furtherance of man's action and course which proceeds from the deity.'[4]

There is a creative tension in the ministry of blessing. We are encouraged to bless others but always in reliance on the fact that it is God who actually blesses. The Bible teaches us that we do not have by right of our being human the sole capacity to pronounce blessings but that we do have a commission to bless under the guidance and authority of God.

There are basically three types of *berakhot* prayers:

1 Those recited before enjoying a material pleasure: *berakhot ha-na' ah.*
2 Those recited before performing a commandment: *berkhot ha-mitzvot.*
3 Those recited at special times and events: *berakhot hoda' ah.*

Berakhot *before enjoying a material pleasure*

These prayers would include blessings for such things as eating and drinking or wearing new clothes. At their heart is the acknowledgement that God is the provider and creator of the thing we are about to use. An example of this are the four blessing prayers of Havdalah that are said to mark the ending of the Shabbat. They are prayed one hour after sunset.

1 Since Havdalah is recited over a cup of wine, the blessing on the wine is said: 'Blessed are You, Lord our God, King of the universe, who creates the fruit of the vine.' Then spices are smelled, preceded by the blessing on smelling spices.
2 'Blessed are You, Lord our God King of the universe, Who creates varieties of spices.' The spices are then passed around and smelled by those present.
3 Next a multi-branched candle that has already been lit is viewed, preceded by the blessing: 'Blessed are You, Lord our God, King of the universe, Who creates the lights of the fire.'
4 Last is a blessing of praise for God's separating the holy from the everyday. 'Blessed are You, Lord our God, King of the universe, Who distinguishes between the sacred and the secular, between light and dark, between Israel and the nations, between the seventh day and the six days of labour. Blessed are You, Lord, Who distinguishes between the sacred and the secular.'

Many of these blessing prayers come with various ritual actions that may seem removed from our modern society but once explored yield a richness of faith and hoped-for outcomes. For example, during the festive meal of Rosh Hashanah there are blessing prayers for apples and honey. The prayer is accompanied by dipping raw apple slices into honey and then blessing it with the words 'Blessed are You, Lord our God, King of the universe, Who creates the fruit of the tree.' The reasoning behind this is that it is symbolic of asking God to grant a sweet new year. Incidentally, once the blessing prayer is prayed, the apple and honey is quickly consumed!

We have considered blessing prayers offered in the synagogue but there is the prayer after meals that is to be prayed at home. This stems from the command of Deuteronomy 8.10–11: 'When you have eaten and are satisfied, praise the LORD your God for the good land he has given you. Be careful that you do not forget the LORD your God' (NIV). It is interesting that it is linked not only to thanks for the satisfying meal but also to recognizing that it is the Lord who provides and that this is the bedrock for our lifestyle and worship of the God who supports us. It is also implicit that such thankfulness is linked to witness and sharing of God's presence and faithfulness to us. In her website article on Judaism, Tracey R. Rich points out that this grace after the meal is usually linked with *berakhot* prayers said before the same meal. There are four in total, and they focus on blessings for the food to be eaten, the blessing of the land itself, which is linked to thankfulness for being brought out of captivity in Egypt, the blessing for the rebuilding of the city of Jerusalem and the blessing for being good and doing good. We are back to that incentive to follow through on the food that is doing us good so that we can go out and do good to others. This is highly evangelistic.[5]

Berakhot *before performing a commandment*

The words of this prayer are 'Blessed are You, Lord our God, King of the universe, Who has sanctified us with His commandments and commands us.' This would be followed by the particular ritual command in question, such as the washing of hands or the lighting of a candle. Such blessing prayers can apply within the home as well as in synagogue services. In the case of the washing of hands before a meal at home it is almost as if the one offering the prayer is the priest and the meal table the altar. Also, the detail surrounding the process of blessing is considerable. You must make sure that the water used in the washing of the hands reaches the entire surface of the hands, so all rings must be removed. The only exception is if a ring is worn permanently and never removed, and so regarded as part of the hand. Rabbi Chabad says that the water is to be poured three times over both hands and that we must make sure it reaches the wrist bone. The fingers are to be separated to allow the water in between them. Rabbi Chisda says, 'Don't skimp! Fill your hands with water and God will fill them with His goodness.'[6]

It is at this point that the blessing prayer is offered, with the hands held chest high, following which they are rubbed together and dried. No speech is allowed until some of the meal following is consumed. As elaborate as this may sound it is more than likely that Jesus was raised on this tradition and that it formed the backcloth to those times we read of his blessing bread and wine, both at the Last Supper and at the conclusion of the Emmaus walk. Such *berakhot* blessings served as a sacramental bridge or touching place in which the ordinary became the venue for the presence of the God of the universe to be realized and experienced once again. This is an important reminder for us today as we have tended to separate the presence of God from the prayers of blessing for the everyday things we enjoy and do. We fail to see God in the ordinary and miss its wonders. Michael Mayne, the former Dean of Westminster Abbey, endeavoured to awake our imagination to this in his book *This Sunrise of Wonder*.[7]

Berakhot *for special times and events*

These prayers cover a wide range of occasions, ranging from seeing a rainbow, thankfulness for the birth of a child, the fruits of harvest, hearing bad news or seeing the king. Basically they remind us that God is the ultimate source and controller of all things bad and good. The *berakhot* for experiencing bad things is 'Blessed are You, Lord our God, King of the Universe, Who is the Judge of truth.' This is not to give thanks for bad things or to say that God deliberately caused such bad things, but a recognition that no matter how bad some things get, God will work his just purposes out through them because nothing is beyond his reach. So in such times we bless the Lord our God so that he will support and hold us through the pain of the present and see us into the hope of the future.

Some years ago a friend called James More Molyneux, a descendant of St Thomas More, told me he was in the habit of blessing his milking cows. James said it was in his interest to do this as the milk went into producing the famous Loseley ice cream. He was passionate about excellence, wanting to give his customers the best he could. He took seriously the blessings mentioned in Deuteronomy, especially those referring to farm produce. No doubt the background to some of his prayers was the raging foot and mouth disease ravaging the UK at that time. He said that some members of his family thought him eccentric, but their huge farm was not affected by the blight and no one can argue that his produce is not among the finest quality in the country.

John J. Parsons says that the blessing prayer on seeing a king lies behind the response of the public when they witnessed the healing miracles of Jesus.[8] This *berakhot* is 'Blessed are You, Lord our God, King of the universe, Who has given of his glory to flesh and blood.' Parsons sees this blessing in the words of the crowd as recorded in Matthew 9.1–8. When they saw Jesus heal the paralytic 'they were filled with awe; and they praised God, who had given such authority to man' (v. 8). He suggests that in seeing Jesus heal so powerfully they were recognizing that he was the expected Messiah or king to come.

Conclusion

We can see that *berakhot* prayers offer a rich rhythm of connection between us and God in the everyday things of life as well as the significant occasions through which we pass. As such they are the backcloth to the prayer life of Jesus and the Church that grew out of his ministry. Studying them gives us new insights to the importance of blessing because they provide us with the drawbridge across which we walk and meet the God who has promised to be always with us. They challenge us to wake up to the power of blessings and rediscover the intimate presence of God in all we do. In Jewish tradition the faithful are encouraged to pray 100 *berakhot* prayers a day. I wonder if this lies behind the exhortation of the Apostle Paul when he wrote to the Ephesian church, 'Blessed be the God and Father of our Lord Jesus Christ, who has blessed us in Christ with every spiritual blessing in the heavenly places' (Eph. 1.3 NRSV).

The blessing prayers of Jesus

We have already referred to Jesus as the principal blesser in the New Testament. We shall now take a closer look at these occasions and unpack the content or effect intended by these blessings. I believe that one simple but profound outcome is that, where appropriate, we are to go and do likewise. As disciples of Jesus we are to learn from him and adopt his ways. We should be blessers too!

The blessing of little children (Mark 10.13–16)

> People were bringing little children to Jesus for him to place his hands on them, but the disciples rebuked them. When Jesus saw this, he was he was indignant. He said to them, 'Let the little children come to me, and do not hinder them, for the kingdom of God belongs to such as these. Truly I tell you, anyone who will not receive the kingdom of God like a little child will never enter it.' And he took the children in his arms, placed his hands on them and blessed them.

Blessing prayers for children already existed in the Jewish community and largely consisted of aspirations that they, the children, would be like and as good as honourable ancestors such as Ephraim and Manasseh, Sarah and Rebecca. To this would be added spontaneous words of prayer. Jesus, however, links the blessing of children to the ability to receive the kingdom of God in your heart. In what is painted as a very intimate scene in which Jesus gathers the children into his arms, he blesses them with this in mind. The actual words are not recorded but I think we are to conclude that his blessing prayer was that they would experience the kingdom of God for themselves. We need to take seriously this link between the prayer of blessing and an expected outcome.

I remember when I was serving as a curate at Christ Church, Walmsley in Bolton. Before this my experience of praying over children too young to receive the Holy Communion was nil. On Parade Sundays when our normal service was overwhelmed with Cubs, Brownies, Guides and Scouts, we had a host of children come to the Communion rail to be blessed. I took part with all the clergy on our team in going among them, row on row, praying short blessings before they returned to their seats. After a few months of this I began to feel that we were short-changing the children because we repeated the same phrase over them all as we glided by them saying, 'The Lord bless you'. I thought that as this was the only time they were in church that Sunday and perhaps for the whole month, they were not getting much out of the experience. So with the permission of my very understanding training incumbent, Fred Cooke, I decided to personalize my blessing prayer for each one of them. I also felt that being over six feet tall I should kneel before them and look them straight in the eye when I prayed. I realized at the same time that I had to keep it short but make it meaningful. Over time I got to know their names and something of their family situation and so made sure that when I blessed I included specific reference to this. I was so encouraged when the children would come to me and say thank you as it had meant much more to them that I took time to pray and made it a little different for everyone. Some were amazed that these little prayers were answered with healing or changes for the better in their homes.

I have to say that I found this exhausting but very rewarding. If we bless with a clear focus and objective we often get better results than just repeating well-intentioned words. I am convinced that this is what Jesus did when he blessed those children. He wanted them to be open to receive the kingdom of God there and then. So the lesson from this example, as from all his blessing prayers, is that Jesus blessed with a clear objective and outcome in mind. We must learn to do the same.

The blessing at the Last Supper (Matthew 26.26–29; Mark 14.22–26; Luke 22.14–23)

> And as they were eating, Jesus took bread, blessed and broke it, and gave it to them and said, 'Take, eat; this is My body.' Then He took the cup, and when He had given thanks He gave it to them, and they all drank from it. And He said to them, 'This is My blood of the new covenant, which is shed for many.'
>
> (Mark 14.22–24 NKJV)

The background to these blessing prayers is twofold: the Passover celebrations and the Feast of Unleavened Bread in which they are held; and the *berakhot* prayers we have already reviewed. William Barclay in his commentary on Matthew gives full details of the Passover ritual and says that Jesus utilized and adapted it to suit his prophetic and pastoral purposes. In particular he is referring to the final consummation of the remaining unleavened bread and the following prayers of thanksgiving, the petition for the coming of Elijah and the blessing prayer over the third cup, called the cup of thanksgiving, that is then drunk.[9] This blessing or *berakhot* prayer would have been the familiar 'Blessed are You, Lord our God, King of the universe, Who creates the fruit of the vine.'

Interestingly the word used by Matthew and Mark for the prayer over the bread is 'blessing' (according to the original Greek text and as reflected in the King James Version), and for the prayer over the wine, 'thanksgiving' or 'celebrate', from which this meal has derived the name of Eucharist. The Apostle Paul used the same two words in his record of the Last Supper in 1 Corinthians 11. He underlines the importance of these words when he says that he received the form of this meal directly from Jesus (1 Cor. 11.23). Most scholars say that we should see that these words have the same weight of meaning and that we should not make any difference of meaning between them. However, we must not lose sight of the nature of biblical blessing, which is the expectancy that in doing this we gain some tangible outcome from God.

There is also a holy rhythm here reflecting the heart of God. Simply stated it is that 'Jesus blesses what is broken and celebrates what gives life.' It is also a prophetic prefiguring of his impending death and resurrection. Whatever is broken or wounded in us, if surrendered to God, can become a stepping stone to blessing either for ourselves or through us for others. Jacob's semi-crippled status after the personal wrestling with God at Jabok caused him to limp, but because he surrendered his life through this encounter, he is rebirthed as Israel, as one who would be a blessing to his generations and even Pharaoh himself. The giving of thanks or celebration over the wine reflects the commitment of Jesus to celebrate what gives life or renewal in or through us. Consider how he celebrated the widow woman who gave everything she had into the Temple treasury, and although no one apparently recognized her gift, he did, and gave thanks for it (Mark 12.41–44). So we can see that this particular meal blessing in that upper room, while having prophetic reference for the death of Jesus, also instils in us a rhythm of consecration and generosity towards our own limitations and brokenness and the good effects of honouring the giftedness we see in others.

What is startling, however, about Jesus' celebration of Passover is that he reshapes the prayers to focus on himself as the new Passover lamb inaugurating a new covenant with God.

In doing this he transports his disciples from the home-based celebration of Passover to the fact that he is bringing in a new relationship with God based not on law but on love. Jesus knew that the cross lay before him, but also that he would rise in resurrection glory. For ever afterwards when the people of God gathered to re-enact this event, he would be present to bless and encourage.

This is not the place to focus on the various theological ideas relating to locating Jesus in the bread and wine themselves but to emphasize the link between the power of blessing prayers and the God who acts on them.

The blessing of the meal at Emmaus (Luke 24.13–35)

> When he was at the table with them, he took bread, blessed and broke it, and gave it to them. Then their eyes were opened, and they recognized him; and he vanished from their sight.
>
> (Luke 24.30–31 NRSV)

It is in the informal intimacy of the meal that Jesus is recognized for who he is rather than in the soul-stirring exposition of Scripture on the road to Emmaus, although the latter prepared the disciples for the former. Some scholars say that Jesus is identified by the wounds in his hands as he blessed the bread and handed it to the disciples. However, these were not the only wounds Jesus carried, and the disciples did not seem to notice them on the road. Darrell Bock says that one of the major themes of Luke the Evangelist is the connection between resurrection appearances and the fellowship meal.[10] For him, the recognition of Jesus is intimately connected with the familiar action of blessing and distributing bread that would take the disciples back to the feeding of the 5,000 and the Last Supper. I think this is at least true, but we must not underestimate the power of blessing. As we have seen from the Last Supper, Jesus has forever altered the impact of blessing the bread to be a proclamation that he is the saviour of the world. In this normal home setting, presumably the home of Cleopas and possibly his wife, who shared that walk, Jesus takes the familiar *berakhot* prayer expected and imbues it with a new authority – it is this that opens their eyes to his identity.

Once again we see the link between the blessing prayer and the outcome of being touched by God is some particular way that he authorizes.

The blessing of the Ascension (Luke 24.50–51)

> When he had led them out to the vicinity of Bethany, he lifted up his hands and blessed them. While he was blessing them, he left them and was taken up into heaven.

This is the final blessing prayer of Jesus in the Gospels, and we do not know what he actually said. However, according to Luke the effect was to produce worship and witness in the lives of the disciples. Augustine said that when the Ascension of Jesus comes to life for us, everything else in the Christian faith will also acquire a new and vital significance. There will be a new purpose or profit in all the Christian festivals and a new power in our personal Christianity.[11] Matthew connects this event in his Gospel with the giving of authority to go out into all the world and make disciples and grow them before the return of Jesus. It is often called the

Great Commission, which gathers up all the previous commissions before it (Matt. 28.18–20). Roy Lawrence, in his classic book on the Ascension, says that it is the preparatory link to the coming of Pentecostal power.[12]

In other words the final blessing prayer of Jesus seems to be focused on the imparting of power and authority to become those who are entitled to go out and share the good news of Jesus. This was certainly taken to heart in the worship response on the mountain of Ascension as well as the patient and anticipatory waiting for the Spirit to come and make it real in that upper room in Jerusalem. Once again the dynamic link between blessing prayer and tangible outcome is underlined.

It is this conferring of authority and power to Christian disciples that forms the basis of our commission to also be the people that bless. The Ascension blessing of Jesus becomes our invitation, under the anointing of that promised Pentecost, to take up this ministry of blessing and exercise it.

One tradition within the Christian faith that has taken this link to heart is that of the Celtic communities that flourished in the British Isles and Brittany between the fifth and eighth centuries.

The Celtic model of blessing prayers

Over the last 25 years we have seen a revival of interest in the legacies of what has been called the Celtic church, although no such church actually existed. More accurately we are referring to the synthesis of Christian faith in the life and culture of the Celtic peoples and the particular ways they shared their witness. The interest is partly fuelled by the desire to get as close as possible to the way of being Church that the earliest Christians in these islands displayed, and to find current ways of being Church today that grow from these tribal roots. There have been at least two major communities formed out of this passion: the Northumbria Community and the Community of Aidan and Hilda. Both have produced liturgies and resources for those who wish to adopt a contemporary lifestyle on the Celtic model.[13]

One of the striking features of the Celtic Christians was the rhythm of blessing that was threaded throughout their witness. As Professor Ian Bradley writes:

> You cannot read far in the lives of the Celtic saints without being struck by how often they blessed people, places and everyday objects. Columba, for example, is portrayed by his biographer Adamnan making the sign of the cross and invoking God's blessing on a fruit tree, a block of salt, a pail of milk and small round stone from a river as well as on his monks and on the island of Iona and its inhabitants. Although many of these benedictions were associated with miraculous happenings and transformations, it is clear from what Adamnan writes that Columba also pronounced blessings on people and objects as a matter of routine and that many people made the long and potentially hazardous journey to Iona just to be blessed by the saint.[14]

However, we must not conclude that blessing prayers were limited to mighty saints like Columba. They were woven into the liturgical life of the Church, as the seventh-century Irish manuscript 'The Antiphonary of Bangor' illustrates. In it the Canticle of Blessings calls on all the elements of God's creation to bless the Lord. From the stars in heaven, the showers and dew, clouds, whales and an assortment of beasts to the birds that fly in the sky – all were to bless the Lord.

Another example of the prominence of blessings can be found in the Gaelic prayers and poems from the Hebrides compiled in the late nineteenth century by Alexander Carmichael and entitled the *Carmina Gadelica.*[15] The subject matter includes daily tasks such as lighting the fire, milking the cow and preparing for bed. Straight away you will notice the direct link here with the *berakhot* prayers that cover a similar range of ordinary everyday activities. However, McLean points out that the majority of the blessings and poems are to do with healing.[16]

This focus on blessing prayers is a reflection not only of the pagan Celtic world's belief in the power and force of the spoken word both to heal and to harm but also of the impact of the new medium of the written word that fuelled the excellence of scholarship in Irish monasticism of this period. Ian Bradley presses home from this observation that the blessing was no mere pleasantry or routine greeting to pass the time of day but rather it conveyed in an almost physical sense a portion of God's goodness and grace.[17]

In parallel to this focus on blessing was also an awareness of the spiritual battle in which each Christian is engaged. Consequently their prayers included invocations alongside the blessings to bring them protection from evil. These are sometimes called caim prayers or prayers of encirclement, in which the supplicants imagine God drawing a circle of protection around them so that good is kept within and evil without. Perhaps the best example of these invocation prayers is the Irish one known as St Patrick's Breastplate, which probably dates from the eighth or ninth century.

I rise today
with the power of God to pilot me,
God's strength to sustain me,
God's wisdom to guide me,
God's eye to look ahead for me,
God's ear to hear me,
God's word to speak for me,
God's hand to protect me,
God's shield to defend me,
God's host to deliver me:
From snares of devils,
From evil temptations,
From nature's failings,
From all who wish to harm me,
Far or near,
Alone and in a crowd.

Around me I gather today all these powers
Against every cruel and merciless force
To attack my body and soul,
Against the charms of false prophets,
The black laws of paganism,
The false laws of heretics,
The deceptions of idolatry,
Against spells cast by women, smiths and druids,
And all unlawful knowledge
That harms my body and soul.[18]

This might not be terribly PC by today's standards of gender equality but it illustrates powerfully the pronouncement element of Celtic prayers.

At the heart of these blessing and invocation prayers is the conviction that the earth is the Lord's and everything in it; that creation is a touching place for the presence of God among us; that God's redeeming love is to be found in places and things as much as in people. Consequently, to pronounce blessings on people and places is to invoke the God who is in it all to make such prayers a touching place for his love and grace. Ian Bradley says that we live in a society where many people are crying out for blessing, healing and affirmation because they are frightened, lonely, depressed, lacking in self-esteem or just stressed out.[19] We need therefore to recover this lost ministry of blessing and take it into our hospitals and care homes, to the housebound and to the neglected parts of our towns and cities. We must learn once again to pray blessing prayers over people and places similar to the two examples below.

Mary Mother's love be thine,
Thine be Bridget's love, of kine.
Love of victor Michael fine,
  Their arm around
  Each hour surround.

Thine great goodness of the sea,
Earth's great goodness to thee be,
Thine great goodness heavenly,
  Thy life be strong
  And fruitful long.

Father, give to thee mild grace,
Loving grace of Son embrace,
Spirit's loving grace emplace.
  So laving thee,
  Pow'r-saving thee. (*The Blessing of Life*)[20]

The blessing of God the Father, who brought you together, go on deepening your love for each other:

The blessing of the great Son, Jesus, who has healed you and helped you through the battles and challenges upon your lives, go on making you radiant in grace and praise:

The blessing of the Holy Spirit, who has chosen to give you both life abundantly, go on enriching the gift you are to each other, the embrace you are to your family and friends and call out of you the gifts and callings he wants you to be for others.

And this we bless to you in the name of the Father and the Son and the Holy Spirit. Amen.

(*Blessing for the renewal of marriage vows*, Russ Parker)

3

The Aaronic blessing prayer

> The LORD bless you and keep you;
> the LORD make his face shine on you and be gracious to you;
> the LORD turn his face toward you and give you peace.
> (Numbers 6.24–26)

This is perhaps the best-known blessing prayer in the world. It has a long history within the daily cycle of Jewish worship services and is often used as a benediction within Christian liturgies. It is also known as the Priestly Blessing because within Judaism it is only the priest who may perform this prayer. Another name for it is 'The Raising of the Hands'. This is because the priest raises his hand over the people as he blesses them, ensuring that his fingers are pressed together while leaving gaps between them so as to form the Hebrew letter 'shin', which stands for almighty God. As this is a holy name it was the usual practice of the worshippers to cover their faces when the priest raised his hands. Yet this configuration of the fingers was popularized on TV by the Hollywood actor Leonard Nimoy, who was raised as a traditional Jew. He used this hand gesture for his Vulcan salute in the popular *Star Trek* series, and accompanied it with the words 'Live long and prosper', which is not far from the intention of the original Aaronic blessing.

This powerful blessing prayer is found in the book of Numbers, which seems to be all about getting ready to live in the land of promise and fulfilment. The background to Numbers is the journey of the Israelites from the Sinai Desert to the steppes of Moab by the River Jordan at the eastern boarder of Canaan. Roy Gane likens the focus of Numbers to the marriage that follows the wedding vows.[1] He says that after the wedding at Sinai where God proclaimed the covenant vows (Ten Commandments) with awesome splendour, Israel said 'I do', and built a house (sanctuary) together and there was a journey through the wilderness of real life.[2] The Aaronic blessing is the articulating of the romance and celebration of God with his bride and the beginning of a new, permanently binding relationship. For better or worse they were now committed to this unique marriage with God that would take them on a journey through the trials of the desert to the land of promised blessings.

Amid the highs and lows of faithfulness and rebellion narrated in Numbers are the laws and promises designed to grow and benefit the new covenant community of faith. We must not lose sight of the fact that these laws and principles for community have as their focus the life that is to be lived in the land of promise. They are not intended for survival in the desert wanderings that resulted from the disobedience of Israel. The challenge for Christians today is to find the enduring principles from this account that hold true for the building of Christ-centred community in the world we occupy. Consequently we need to discover and utilize the place of blessing prayers for this quest of faith and witness.

Many of the chapters in Numbers begin with the statement 'The Lord said to Moses', which is intended to contrast with the giving of laws on the Mount at Sinai, only they are given to Moses in the Tent of Meeting. The giving of the laws on the mountain takes the form of a prescription for community living whereas the words given personally to and via Moses underline his function as the one elected to speak with the authority of God. In other words the injunction to bless comes with the authority to do so. This particular blessing prayer comes as the command of God via Moses to Aaron (Num. 6.22–23). Once again we notice that when the blessing is given it is pronounced with authority and not prayed for as a request.

The purpose of this blessing: to renew the community of faith

This blessing concludes with the words 'So they will put my name on the Israelites, and I will bless them.' We must not lose sight of the fact that it was not long before the writing of this blessing that the whole community of the Israelites was on the verge of losing its entire identity and destiny. It was still fresh in the memory that the community that had seen miracles of deliverance from bondage in Egypt had almost overnight abandoned this saving God and returned to worshipping the gods of their oppressors in the form of the golden calf (Exod. 32.1–33). The seeming ringleader of this debacle is Aaron himself, who is painted as the pawn of the mob who instigated the revolt. It is therefore a miracle of grace that it is God who instructs Moses to tell Aaron that it is his calling to give this blessing prayer. What an outstanding restoration from the grace and mercy of God!

However, although forgiveness is given after judgement, there arises the crucial issue of whether God's presence or name would remain among them. We are told in Exodus 33 that God indeed would keep his promise and ensure that they successfully entered the promised land, but now he would send the angel of the Lord to accompany them. He himself would not be going up with them.

Think of it: God was offering his best angel and guaranteeing the Israelites that all their dreams will be fulfilled – the death of their enemies and conquest and settlement in a land flowing with milk and honey. Many of us might easily settle for such guarantees from the God of heaven – but not Moses. All through his ministry he had done his best to stay focused on the importance of covenant identity: that the Israelites were the called community of God, and to remain as such they could not be parted from his presence, not even by a mighty angel. And so Moses says to God, 'If your Presence does not go with us, do not send us up from here' (Exod. 33.15).

To go with the presence of God is true Emmanuel living. Consequently, when Numbers 6.27 states that the purpose of the Aaronic blessing was to put the name of God on the community, it was to renew that community in its walk with God. It was to make real and more effective the power and presence of God so that our testimony demonstrates that God is with this people.

So we learn from this background context that the Aaronic blessing prayer is no mere utterance of hoped-for nice things but a powerful renewing of our call to be the people on whom God has placed his signature name and presence and a reminder that all we do reflects this reality. With this in mind, let us now look in more detail at the structure and content of the blessing.

The shape of blessings to come

The shape of this blessing is typical of Hebrew poetry where the same goal – putting God's name back on the people of faith – is expressed in three parallel statements.

First statement: 'The Lord bless you and keep you'

In his Commentary on Numbers, Norman Snaith says that the word for 'keep' can also mean 'preserve', 'guard' or 'care for'.[3] This makes clear that it is God who is blessing, even though it is being pronounced by Aaron.

Second statement: 'The Lord make his face shine on you and be gracious to you'

It is interesting to know that the Greek Septuagint Bible uses the word 'epiphany' here, and it brings out the dynamic force intended in the original Hebrew word of 'shining out'. Snaith says that this is not a steady, continuous shining but an ever-renewed access of light – not a state so much as an action. The phrase indicates outgoing activity in goodwill.[4] God's shining revelation is to do us good and bring us to intimacy and not mere association with his cause.

The face of a person becomes synonymous with the presence of the person, and so the Hebrew expression used here, *lip'ne*, means 'to the face of' and 'in front of'.[5] In other words it refers to intimacy and closeness of friends. So this priestly blessing is designed to inspire and increase intimacy and unity of fellowship between God and whoever is being blessed. This is in fact exactly how the friendship between God and Moses is described. It was in the rhythm of their relationship when the pillar of cloud or fire appeared that Moses would come to the front of his tent, and it was then that God spoke with him face to face as one speaks to a friend (Exod. 33.11).

It may be just a matter of semantics, but we do need to note that this face to face encounter was God's initiative. When Moses desired to see God's glory or face it was not granted to him. Moses is told that to look upon the face of God is to perish, so we read that he veils his face as he hides in the cleft of a rock, and God covers him with the veil of his hand while his glory passes by (Exod. 33.20–23). It is this limitation that is picked up in the New Testament when Paul assures his readers that in the last days we will come to complete maturity in our faith and we will be able to see God face to face in Christ (1 Cor. 13.12; 2 Cor. 4.6). John the Divine in writing Revelation goes even further when he describes the face of Jesus as shining like the sun in all its brilliance (Rev. 1.16). You wonder if he is thinking back to that other shining moment on the Mount of Transfiguration when Jesus stood in dazzling fullness before them, or possibly that unique event of Jesus' Ascension when he was gathered into glory and surrounded by angels (Mark 9.2–3; Acts 1.9–11). Certainly seeing God face to face is an important fulfilment for John. In his final chapter he paints the picture of life for the redeemed community upon the new earth. The throne of God is set up at the heart of this new society and as all curses of the past are broken and the Lamb now reigns in the city, this new community is empowered to see God's face and come together in a consummation of blessings (Rev. 22.4). For John the curse of the golden calf that threatened the Israelite community with loss of identity and purpose is now shattered as God brings all the faithful into the new community of those who literally wear the sacred name of God on their foreheads.

Roy Gane says that where this blessing speaks of God being gracious to us it does not mean that God merely smiles at us. He says that to be gracious means to show favour in the form of beneficial action.[6] Compare the following examples:

> Then Esau looked up and saw the women and children. 'Who are these with you?' he asked. Jacob answered, 'They are the children God has graciously given your servant.' (Genesis 33.5)

> [David] answered, 'While the child was still alive, I fasted and wept. I thought, 'Who knows? The Lord may be gracious to me and let the child live.' (2 Samuel 12.22)

Both Jacob and David interpreted the graciousness of God in practical outcomes, namely the provision of living children. This gives strength to the whole concept of blessing being something with its focus on a solid expectation of a tangible outcome and not just the expressing of praiseworthy and commendable sentiments. For it to be a genuine blessing it had to be married to an outcome that could be measured and experienced.

Third statement: 'The Lord turn his face toward you and give you peace'

According to the Sifra (the Halakic Midrash commentary to the book of Leviticus), to lift up the countenance or turn the face towards means to turn away from anger and to show favour.[7] When God spoke to Moses in the tent of meeting to announce his imminent death, he revealed to Moses what he could see in the future story of the people of Israel. He informs Moses that they will indeed enter the land of promise but that it was only a matter of time before they would rebel and forsake their covenant commitments again. God's response to this was to say to Moses, 'In that day I will become angry with them . . . I will hide my face from them, and they will be destroyed' (Deut. 31.17). Once again we see the shadow of the golden calf surrounding this blessing.

In fact throughout the Old Testament there is the parallel cry of the heart either for God to shine his face in blessing on his people or the question of why God is no longer doing so. Invariably the latter is a sign of God's anger or judgement on a people who have broken their covenant walk with him – they are reaping what they have sown.

'Why do you hide your face?'

Job asks God this question because he felt God had turned against him and was punishing him by destroying his family, fortune and health (Job 13.24; cf. 34.29).

King David frequently cried out to God with this searching question as he was struggling with depression and as his life was under constant threat (Ps. 13.1; cf. 27.9, 44.24, 69.17, 88.14, 102.2, 143.7).

Most of the classical prophets, such as Isaiah, Jeremiah and Ezekiel, use this expression of God turning his face away to describe divine judgement in the light of national apostasy (Isa. 54.8; 57.17; Jer. 33.5; Ezek. 7.22).

'Let the light of your face shine on us'

David was not shy to ask why God had turned his face away, but neither was he slow to invite God to turn his face towards him and give him favour. A typical example is Psalm 4.6–7, where he says, 'Let the light of your face shine on us. Fill my heart with joy when their grain and new wine abound.' It seems he also knew when to party with God![8] Other examples all contain similar aspirations to the Aaronic blessing.

Finally there are the exhortations from God himself for his people to seek his face in order to secure his favour and continued blessings in their lives. One of the most famous examples of this comes during the dedication of the First Temple when the congregation of God is encouraged to 'turn from their wicked ways' and seek the face of God so that they would not be judged but blessed (2 Chron. 7.14). In rebuilding the broken community of faith, King Hezekiah writes a letter to the nation encouraging them to return to a righteous walk with God, saying that if they do this then God would show himself to be gracious and compassionate and not turn his face from them (2 Chron. 30.9). This is surely what is in the mind of Paul when he encourages the dysfunctional Corinthian church to stay steadfast in its faithful obedience to Jesus because the end of this journey will result in seeing the glory of God in the face of their saviour Jesus the Messiah (2 Cor. 4.6).

'And give you peace'

The word for peace here is the very familiar word 'Shalom'. It is often translated as 'peace' but its basic meaning is completeness and total welfare. Roy Gane reminds us that well-being is directly connected with the bread of the presence placed on the golden table in the outer sanctuary (Lev. 24.5–9; 1 Kings 7.48). Gane points out that a component of well-being is the daily sustenance of food represented by the bread.[9]

Gane also makes an interesting comparison between the Aaronic blessing and the three middle requests that Jesus makes in the Lord's Prayer. He sees what he calls a chiastic or crossword connection if we link up the first request in the Aaronic blessing with the last in the Lord's Prayer, and the third in the former with the first in the latter. Also, the middle sections are directly connected. The text diagram below illustrates this.[10]

<table>
<tr><td>The Lord bless you and keep [or guard] you</td><td>The Lord turn his face toward you and give you peace</td></tr>
<tr><td>Lead us not into temptation but deliver us from the evil one</td><td>Give us today our daily bread</td></tr>
</table>

The Lord make his face shine on you and be gracious to you

Forgive us our debts

Granted this may be merely an interesting observation, it does raise the question of whether Jesus' prayer was modelled on the priestly blessing of Aaron; and if so, it echoes the quest both to give and receive the power of God's blessings. W. H. Bellinger says that the Aaronic blessings contain verbs in the command or jussive tense.[11] This is in keeping with what we have so far understood about the nature of giving blessings: they are not prayed for but pronounced. The three prayer requests in the heart of the disciples' prayer are also in this command tense: give us, forgive us and lead us not but deliver us! So it seems we could say that the Lord's Prayer, which is such a fundamental part of the Church's liturgies, needs to be revised somewhat in our estimation. We need to see that it contains the aspirations of pronouncing requests and outcomes that are at the very heart of what it is to bless.

The purpose of this blessing: to put God's name on his people

Moses may not have seen the face of God but he did receive the name of God on his body and life, and this brings us back to the purpose of this Aaronic blessing. If we keep in mind once again that this blessing comes in the shadow of the recent memory of abandoning faith in God through flaunting the golden calf, we will appreciate all the more the significance of its purpose. That purpose is to restore what was lost in the rebellion in the wilderness; it is to give back to the restored community the assurance that God was with them, which was signalled by the placing of the name of God over them.

The word 'name' was used in antiquity as a substitute for the actual divine name itself. To know a person's name was to have power over or influence with him. When Jacob finally surrendered to God after a tumultuous wrestle for supremacy, God gives him the new name of Israel because it signifies a divine struggle that resulted in Jacob overcoming his own dysfunctional nature (Gen. 32.28–29).

A person's name often signified character. For example Jacob, whose name translates as 'supplanter' or 'schemer', is seen to live the life that his name indicates. Similarly God's name represents his character of holiness, well-being and truth. Consequently the Israelites are encouraged to worship only in the places and according to instructions that God gives, and if they do then they will be blessed with well-being and abundance of crops and freedom from their enemies (Deut. 12.5–7, 11, 21).

We can see now that for the Israelites to rebel against God was to risk his anger, but more importantly to lose the benefits of the name of God being their identity marker and preserver. This is why among the Ten Commandments we have the injunction not to 'misuse the name of the LORD your God' (Exod. 20.7).

As the people of Israel prepare to move on into the promised land following the debacle of the golden calf, Moses tells God that he would rather not go on if the presence of God is not going with them. God had offered them the company of a mighty angel who would help them gain all their objectives of conquering this new land. And so God reassures Moses that his presence will indeed go with them. He says, 'I will cause all my goodness to pass in front of you, and I will proclaim my name, the LORD, in your presence' (Exod. 33.19). This was the welcomed promise that they were to be once again the people who carry Yahweh's name and favour.

I see a real connection between this event and the words in the Lord's Prayer, 'Hallowed be your name' (Matt. 6.9). This is the Christian cry that God through Jesus keeps his name and almighty presence on us so that we live in the well-being and wholeness of God's blessings. Similarly when others come to us with gifts from God through word and action, we recognize the touch of God's prophetic presence in their ministry by saying, 'Blessed is he who comes in the name of the Lord' (Matt. 21.9).

Giving away the Aaronic blessing

We began this chapter by reminding ourselves that the original use of this prayer was exclusive to Aaron in his role as the high priest of the community, and that it forms part of the regular prayer life of Jewish synagogues to this day. While not undermining the importance of this history, we do need to ask ourselves as Christians whether we too can become the people who bless others in this way. Both the First Epistle of Peter and the book of Revelation give some attention to the new status of Christians concerning their service to God and the world, and it is that of being a kingdom of priests. Peter describes this priesthood as both holy and royal (1 Pet. 2.5, 9). The three references in Revelation speak of this priesthood being offered to God but also connects it with the rule and ministry of God on the earth (Rev. 1.6; 5.10; 20.6). While this priesthood does not refer to the Old Testament priestly status or function within the sacrificial system, it does take the principle of priesthood as being the people who stand between the holiness of God and the needs of the community. It is for this reason alone that we need to take the ministry of blessing seriously and rediscover ways God calls us to give his blessings to the people whose needs we serve.

One such example of this is the story of the community of Ffald-y-Brenin in south-west Wales. In the early days of establishing their community, the founders became aware of the suspicions of and distancing by the farmers and folk surrounding them. Many were critical of there being a Christian centre among them. Roy and Daphne Godwin began a slow and patient dialogue with their neighbours and in so doing began to learn of their difficulties and concerns – poverty and loss of income through harsh winters when crops failed and livestock perished in the snows. It was this awareness that challenged them to come alongside their community with prayers of blessing. Their prayers were not intercessions but pronouncements that took form in something like the following:

> In the name of Jesus Christ our Lord we bless you with abundant crops in all seasons. We bless your cattle and sheep that they will be healthy and that none will be lost through bad, winter weather. We bless you with the favour of God in your homes and in your business. Amen.

Over time, according to Roy, some of the local farmers began to report that business was improving and that rather than poor returns from their fields they were experiencing a good output of crops. Others said they had never known years when their cattle and sheep were so healthy. Gradually new friendships were forged, and when Ffald-y-Brenin was looking for extra accommodation for people attending their centre, the local farmers began a new ministry of bed and breakfasts. This brought new business in the lean months to this area, and many have gained a new respect both for Ffald-y-Brenin and the Christian faith.

I think we can learn from this experience and find ways to discern the needs of our community and add to our usual intercessions the blessing prayers of faith through which we focus the touch of God to meet our community at its points of need. Some churches now actively encourage their members to prayer-walk the streets, not looking for something to take on in battle but to bless.

There is not only a missional focus for this blessing prayer but also a pastoral one. This is supremely seen in the blessing pronouncements of Jesus that we call the Beatitudes. We will examine these in our next chapter.

Conclusion

We noted early on in Chapter 1 that the Old Testament, Hebrew word for bless is *barakh* and that it means to bend the knee. Jeff Benner of the Ancient Hebrew Research Centre says that it literally means 'the bringing of a gift to another on bended knee'. When we bless God or others we are in essence bringing a gift on bended knee. However, Benner goes on to say that the Scriptures frequently mention that it is God blessing us or bending the knee. He writes, 'A true king is one who serves his people, one who will humble himself and come to his people on a bended knee!'[12] I think we need to understand this reference in terms of a servant heart rather than servitude or a demeaning of the almightiness of God! Jesus literally took a towel and bent his knee before his disciples in that last upper room, and washed their feet to underline that their true calling was to serve and not to lord it over others. This should also give us another appreciation of the references in Scripture to God being seated on a throne, and we should associate with it not just divine power and status but the king who comes to serve and make us truly human.

Consequently Benner rewrites this Aaronic blessing and gives it a certain freshness. Let us close the chapter with this.

> Yahweh will kneel before you presenting gifts and will guard you with a hedge of protection,
> Yahweh will illuminate the wholeness of his being toward you bringing order and he will beautify you,
> Yahweh will lift up his wholeness of being and look upon you and he will set in place all you need to be whole and complete.[13]

Amen.

4

The blessed state: Jesus and Beatitude blessings

> Jesus is not saying that these are simply timeless truths about the way the world is, about human behaviour . . . Mourners often go uncomforted, the meek don't inherit the earth, those who long for justice frequently take that longing to the grave. This is an upside-down world . . . *and Jesus is saying that with his work it's starting to come true.* This is an announcement, not a philosophical analysis of the world . . . It is *gospel*: good news, not good advice.[1]

You will not find the word 'beatitude' in the Bible. It is the anglicized form of the Greek word *makarios* taken from the Vulgate or Latin version word *beatitudo* in Matthew's Gospel. In particular the word refers to Jesus' pronouncement describing the quality of the life of his kingdom disciples as listed in the Sermon on the Mount (Matt. 5.3–12) and the parallel account in Luke's Gospel called the Sermon on the Plain (6.20–23). Matthew lists eight Beatitudes and Luke four, with four accompanying woes (6.24–26).

As we have noted before, *makarios* is basically interpreted as 'happy'. William Barclay says that the term is more of an exclamation than a statement. As the verb 'to be' does not exist in Greek, he says that this expression, originally uttered by Jesus in Aramaic, would be very similar to other Old Testament exclamations of blessing and should be rendered, 'O the blessedness of (the poor in spirit)'. He insists that Beatitudes are congratulations on what is now the experience of the blessed.[2]

Barclay compares the Beatitudes of Jesus with similar references from the Psalms.

> Blessed are those who do not walk in step with the wicked or stand in the way that sinners take or sit in the company of mockers, but who delight in the law of the LORD and meditate on his law day and night. They are like a tree planted by streams of water, which yields its fruit in season and whose leaf does not wither – whatever they do prospers. (Psalm 1.1–3 TNIV)

> Blessed are those whose transgressions are forgiven, whose sins are covered. Blessed are those whose sin the LORD does not count against them and in whose spirit is no deceit. (Psalm 32.1–2 TNIV)

In pressing home his point, Barclay goes further in saying that a correct interpretation of this expression in modern terminology would be the exclamation 'O the bliss!'[3] This contrasts sharply with the rather poor translation of *makarios* as 'happy'. The English word 'happiness' contains the root *hap*, which means chance. Human happiness is dependent on the chances and changes of life and so can be taken away. The blessed state Jesus declares over his disciples describes that joy that is serene, untouchable and self-contained, that is completely independent of all the chances and changes of life. Christian blessedness is completely untouchable and unassailable – 'No one', said Jesus, 'will take away your joy' (John 16.22). Blessedness is that joy that shines through tears and that nothing in life or death can take away.

However, what is outrageous about the Beatitudes of Jesus is that they are given fulfilment in the context of persecution and suffering – not in the distant future where we might have come through all our troubles and losses but in the here and now. Peter, an undoubted recipient of this teaching, picks up the theme of blessedness in persecution when he writes to the scattered Christian communities in Asia. Here his focus is suffering for the name of Jesus. 'But even if you should suffer for what is right, you are blessed' (1 Pet. 3.14). 'If you are insulted because of the name of Christ, you are blessed, for the Spirit of glory and of God rests on you' (1 Pet. 4.14). This theme of Beatitude endurance is also picked up by James in his great epistle. 'Blessed are those who persevere under trial, because when they have stood the test, they will receive the crown of life that God promised to those who love him' (James 1.12 TNIV). He goes on to liken the endurance of the faithful to Job, who kept his integrity in extreme suffering. 'As you know, we count as blessed those who have persevered. You have heard of Job's perseverance and have seen what the Lord finally brought about' (James 5.11). Job hung on doggedly to the belief that God was utterly present in his sufferings, which gave him heart to speak out his pain in the confidence that God was fully present to him. Both Peter and James understood the sufferings of faith to be the sufferings of Jesus, and that the blessedness to which they referred was the knowledge that Jesus personally shared with his followers the fight of faith they were facing.

An ancient and well-known example of this blessed state under duress was that of Polycarp, the aged Bishop of Smyrna, who was thought to have been a disciple of the Apostle John and appointed by him as bishop. During a time of persecution in the reign of the Emperor Marcus Aurelius (155–67), Polycarp was arrested and sentenced to death by burning in the arena at Smyrna. According to the Martyrdom of Polycarp, when the aged saint was asked to renounce his faith he replied with these famous words: 'Fourscore and six have I served Him, and He hath done me no wrong. How then can I speak evil of my King, who saved me?'[4]

Before proceeding, we need to remind ourselves that these Beatitudes come in the context of the Sermon on the Mount. Some have described the sermon as a mandate for the witness and life of the kingdom community of Jesus. What cannot be forgotten is that the one who preaches this sermon is the Son of God, that he is the Messiah who is making all things new. Accordingly the sermon is the reality of the new age of grace made possible in time.[5] Similarly, Dietrich Bonhoeffer is keen that we do not fall into the trap of separating the sermon from the one who gave it, which is to reduce it to a collection of ideals that only the best of us could scarcely achieve.

The Sermon on the Mount is the word of the one who did not relate to reality as a foreigner, a reformer, a fanatic or the founder of a religion but as one who bore and experienced the nature of reality in his own body, who spoke out of the depth of reality as no other human being on earth before. The sermon is the word of the very one who is the lord and law of reality. It is to be interpreted as the word of God who became human.[6]

The sayings of the Sermon on the Mount are the interpretation of Jesus' life, and that same life is to be the shared experience of his disciples, who live and move and have their being in him. Therefore these Beatitudes, as part of this great sermon life, are not addressed to individuals but to the community that derives its life from being in Christ. They are not a hero ethic but the constitution of the Jesus people. They articulate the lifestyle of those who know that the only way life is going to be lived is in utter dependence on Jesus the Messiah. This is the blessed state.

Stanley Hauerwas picks this up when he says that the Beatitudes are not a list of requirements but are in fact the interpretative key to the kingdom life described in the whole Sermon on the Mount, and as such are descriptive of a people gathered around Jesus.

No one is asked to go out and try to be poor in spirit or to mourn or to be meek. Rather Jesus is indicating that given the reality of the kingdom, we should not be surprised to find among those who follow him those who are poor in spirit, those who mourn, those who are meek. Moreover Jesus does not suggest that everyone who follows him will possess all the Beatitudes, but we can be sure that some will be poor, some will mourn and some will be meek.[7]

Now we do not usually associate being poor in spirit, mourning, meekness, hunger and persecution with blessedness. Hauerwas says that 'blessed' is here signalling that the transformation of the world is now under way through the reigning presence of king Jesus. I think this is the right lens through which to understand the Beatitudes and the blessed state they outline. We do need to resist the temptation to think that being blessed is the reward of some faith endeavour or perseverance on our behalf. Not everyone who has mourned has found the comfort they needed, indeed some have used grief to keep others at a distance. Not all the meek found themselves popular and so elevated to the ranks of land ownership. Not all the hungry have been fed; sadly in these days of pandemic famines many have perished. Not everyone has been able to endure persecutions for right causes.

Origen, the early Greek Father of the church, said that the source for any understanding of the Beatitudes must be Jesus.[8] It is Jesus who is the one who is poor in spirit – the great church hymn of Philippians offers us an early glimpse of this:

Who, being in very nature God,
did not consider equality with God something to be used to his own advantage;

rather, he made himself nothing
by taking the very nature of a servant,
being made in human likeness.
And being found in appearance as a human being,
he humbled himself
by becoming obedient to death –
even death on a cross! (Philippians 2.6–8 TNIV)

This is not to say that our poverty of spirit is the same as Jesus' self-emptying, rather that Jesus' poverty has made it possible for a community to exist who can live dispossessed of their possessions. To be those who live in the blessed state is to be the ones who live in Christ, who surrender their living to him and whose losses are stepping stones to living in this awareness and reality. The blessed state signals those who have recognized their total need of Jesus and whose lives are lived from that cornerstone and perspective. The blessed are those who rejoice in the divine encounter of Christ in them, the hope of glory.

This chapter is not an attempt to give a full commentary on the Beatitudes but to point to the foundational fact of all Christian living and experience, which is that the blessed state reflects the benefits of those who know their total need to live in Jesus.

Having researched a large number of biblical commentaries on the subject, I have been challenged and refreshed by the reflections of William Barclay, which although written over 50 years ago still speak with a sharpness and relevance today. I encourage you therefore to examine the Beatitudes and their implications by looking at the two sets of Beatitudes below, the traditional translations from Scripture and those in Barclay's inimitable style.

1 Blessed are the poor in spirit, for theirs is the kingdom of heaven.
O the bliss of those who have realized their own utter helplessness, and who have put their whole trust in God, for thus alone can they render to God that perfect obedience which will make them citizens of the Kingdom of Heaven!
2 Blessed are those who mourn, for they will be comforted.
O the bliss of those whose hearts are broken for the world's suffering and for their own sin, for out of their sorrow they will find the joy of God!

3 Blessed are the meek, for they will inherit the earth.
O the bliss of those who are always angry at the right time and never angry at the wrong time, who have every instinct, impulse and passion under control because they themselves are God-controlled, who have the humility to realize their own ignorance and their own weakness, for such people can indeed rule the world!
4 Blessed are those who hunger and thirst for righteousness, for they will be filled.
O the bliss of those who long for total righteousness as the starving long for food, and those perishing of thirst long for water, for they will be truly satisfied!
5 Blessed are the merciful, for they will be shown mercy.
O the bliss of those who can get right inside other people, until they can see with their eyes, think with their thoughts, feel with their feelings, for those who do that will find others do the same for them, and will know that that is what God in Jesus Christ has done!
6 Blessed are the pure in heart, for they will see God.
O the bliss of those whose motives are absolutely pure, for they will some day be able to see God!
7 Blessed are the peacemakers, for they will be called the children of God.
O the bliss of those who produce right relationships one with another, for they are doing Godlike work!
8 Blessed are those who are persecuted because of righteousness, for theirs is the kingdom of heaven.
O the bliss of those who are persecuted for their loyalty to God's way of life, for the blessings of the Kingdom of Heaven are theirs here and now![9]

Tom Wright picks up the now and the not yet aspect of the Beatitudes when he says that they are a summons to live in the present in the way that will make sense in God's promised future – because that future has arrived in the present in Jesus of Nazareth.[10]

Blessed in the heavenly realms

> Praise be to the God and Father of our Lord Jesus Christ, who has blessed us in the heavenly realms with every spiritual blessing in Christ. (Ephesians 1.3)

Paul has his own version of the blessed state, and he begins his great letter to the Ephesian church with a reminder that as Christians their true location is of those seated in the heavenly realms. Admittedly Paul's statement refers to spiritual blessings, but we must not think that this indicates some internal holy pursuit or heavenly state of repose. Paul is writing from prison after all! His prime reference is to Jesus Christ. His argument is one of position. He is offering the Ephesians a perspective on their position in Christ as they face the storm of opposition in their secular context.

I suppose the common answer to the often asked question, 'How are you doing?' is to say, 'I am OK under the circumstances.' Paul wants to shift this perspective by reminding his readers that we are actually 'above' the circumstances as we are seated in Christ in the heavenly realm. He is referring to the Beatitude location we have been exploring – that of being in the blessed state for no other reason than as believers we are to be found in Christ. To belong to Jesus is to be in the position of living out the blessings that are to be found in living in Christ. Paul repeats this reference to our heavenly location three more times in his letter.

> That power [which is at work in us] is the same as the mighty strength he exerted when he raised Christ from the dead and seated him at his right hand in the heavenly realms, far above all rule and authority, power and dominion, and every name that is invoked, not only in the present age but also in the one to come. (Ephesians 1.19–21)

> And God raised us up with Christ and seated us with him in the heavenly realms in Christ Jesus. (Ephesians 2.6)

> His intent was that now, through the church, the manifold wisdom of God should be made known to the rulers and authorities in the heavenly realms, according to his eternal purpose that he accomplished in Christ Jesus our Lord.
> (Ephesians 3.10–11)

Two of these references refer to the authority of Christ over the powers abroad that would contend with the Ephesian church's right to live the life it does. Whether these are powers hostile to the rule of Jesus or whether they are corrosive, secular powers that would endeavour to shape the church into its own mould, Paul would have the believers secure in their position of authority to live a holy life in Christ. However,

Paul is also keen to remind the church that by staying in touch with their heavenly location in Christ, they would experience the blessings that come from being so connected to Jesus. This blessed state is none other than the life of Christ Jesus lived out in their community life.

The sevenfold blessings of the book of Revelation

We have seen that the word *makarios* embraces the now and not yet of the tangible benefits of being the people who live in Christ. There is a sense of the future in *makarios* and so it is logical that it should become a part of the discussion of the end times. Both sets of Beatitudes refer to the future consummation of the here-and-now blessings. In the Lucan version Jesus says that the day will come when the faithful will receive the kingdom of God: then they will be filled and will laugh though life at present is not ideal (Luke 6.20–21). Paul in writing to Titus reminds him that the life of faithful endurance and holiness of life is the expression of those awaiting the blessed hope of Christ's final appearing (Titus 2.11–13).

This quality of active waiting and the blessings that it brings forms one of the major strands in the Revelation of Saint John. I do not think it an accident that the reference to the blessed life is mentioned seven times in the text. The design of this seems to underline the completeness or wholeness that the blessed state is to build within our shared lives as a Christian community.

Blessing 1

Blessed is the one who reads aloud the words of this prophecy, and blessed are those who hear it and take to heart what is written in it, because the time is near. (1.3 TNIV)

Blessing 2

I heard a voice from heaven say, 'Write: Blessed are the dead who die in the Lord from now on.' 'Yes,' says the Spirit, 'they will rest from their labour, for their deeds will follow them.' (14.13 TNIV)

Blessing 3

Look, I come like a thief! Blessed are those who stay awake and keep their clothes on, so that they may not go naked and be shamefully exposed. (16.15 TNIV)

Blessing 4

Then the angel said to me, 'Write: Blessed are those who are invited to the wedding supper of the Lamb!' (19.9 TNIV)

Blessing 5

Blessed and holy are those who have part in the first resurrection. The second death has no power over them, but they will be priests of God and of Christ and will reign with him for a thousand years. (20.6 TNIV)

Blessing 6

Look, I am coming soon! Blessed are those who keep the words of the prophecy in this scroll. (22.7 TNIV)

Blessing 7

Blessed are those who wash their robes, that they may have the right to the tree of life and may go through the gates into the city. (22.14 TNIV)

Conclusion

The Beatitude, or blessed state, is therefore the condition of those who live faithfully in Christ. This state is not determined by what we experience so that it is a reward for services rendered. For some, the deepening of this state of being blessed is through the fulcrum of suffering with Christ and for others because they are caught up in the passions and care of Jesus for his broken world.

What they all have in common is a staying true to and connected with the Lord Jesus who first captivated their lives. Consequently the blessed state is to be found in Christ at all times and in all places. This alone is the pearl of great price over which we have such profound joy.

It is also a perfectly acceptable practice to proclaim in recognition those whom we know to be blessed of God. Our proclamations of such do not confer a state of blessedness on anyone but may encourage recipients to dig deeper into the reality of where God's grace and their faith has taken them.

Some years ago I was on a personal pilgrimage visiting Celtic holy sites in the North of England and Scotland. My journey brought me one day to the church of St Paul's in Monkwearmouth, where Bede was once in community at the monastery that stood on this site. As I entered that ancient church I was met by three elderly ladies who were members of the church congregation and who were there to greet any visitors. They offered me a share of their tea and sandwiches, which I gratefully received. While eating they told me something of the story and witness of their community. After eating they then asked me if I would like them to pray for me. I said yes. They led me to the little lady chapel with its ancient stained-glass window. As I knelt, they laid hands on me and prayed such a wonderful prayer that I felt filled with the peace of Christ, and they also had some words of encouragement for me, the stranger among them. Before leaving I turned to them and said, 'You are the blessed people of God because you have brought Jesus to me in a lovely and gentle way.' Their faces lit up and one of them said to me that this was such an encouragement – they felt they were not able to do much in sharing their faith because they were all quite old and did not get out very much, save for this occasional duty for their church. I told them that they probably had no idea of the blessing they were to all who passed through this church, offering welcome and warmth in the name of Jesus. It reminded me of that old and popular revival song:

> When upon life's billows you are tempest-tossed,
> When you are discouraged, thinking all is lost,
> Count your many blessings, name them one by one,
> And it will surprise you what the Lord hath done.
>
> *(Refrain)*
> *Count your blessings, name them one by one,*
> *Count your blessings, see what God hath done!*
> *Count your blessings, name them one by one,*
> *And it will surprise you what the Lord hath done.*
>
> Are you ever burdened with a load of care?
> Does the cross seem heavy you are called to bear?
> Count your many blessings, every doubt will fly,
> And you will keep singing as the days go by.
>
> *(Refrain)*
>
> When you look at others with their lands and gold,
> Think that Christ has promised you His wealth untold;

Count your many blessings wealth can never buy
Your reward in heaven, nor your home on high.

(Refrain)

So, amid the conflict whether great or small,
Do not be discouraged, God is over all;
Count your many blessings, angels will attend,
Help and comfort give you to your journey's end.

(Refrain)[11]

5

Expecting blessings

> If you believe in God, He will open the windows of heaven and pour blessings upon you. (Mahalia Jackson)

I was sitting with friends in the gallery of the Swansea Grand Theatre watching the premiere presentation of the musical *Amazing Grace*, written and presented by another friend, Mal Pope. The musical focused on the Welsh Revival that occurred almost exactly 100 years earlier, when over 100,000 people where swept into the kingdom of God through a massive outpouring of the Holy Spirit. There came a special moment for us all when the song 'Warm Wind' was sung. The song was about the coming of the Spirit on the people of the land who would be touched by the power of God. Some of the words struck a deep chord in my heart. They were: 'There's a warm wind blowing, it's blowing right across my path, it's where I want to be!'

Suddenly all around me I noticed people raising their hands in worship. Some were crying and others were kneeling by their seats. It was quite obvious that the Spirit of God was moving in that theatre and touching hearts and lives. We were in a moment of renewal when the presence of God was felt to be very close and it was changing people. I heard someone seated near me say, 'They are getting God's blessings for them.' It was a special moment that does not come too often in our lives. However, it also brought home to me in a new awareness that whenever God finds us ready and wanting he sends his Holy Spirit to give us the blessings we are ready to live with. In the case of those in the Swansea Grand Theatre that night it was renewed faith in Jesus Christ, and as we later learned, even salvation for many who had simply come to watch a good musical!

In the last chapter we looked at the Beatitudes and the blessings on those who lived with such a God-focused attitude that they were the people God loved to bless. However, in addition to these the

Scriptures record that there are other circumstances or contexts in which we can expect to be blessed by God. These are conditions of living that God has promised to give his blessing to, and if we live them we should become the people who expect to be blessed in them. We must not view these in a cold and calculating way as if they are a formula we can adopt and God has to do our bidding and bless us. They are rather the principles of Godly commissioning by which he delights to bless those who walk in his ways. There are four such principles: the obedience of covenant keeping, living in unity, holy living and saving grace.

The obedience of covenant keeping

If you trawl through the Law Codes of Leviticus and Deuteronomy, what emerges is a blueprint for blessing God's community in the land that he has provided. Here is an example:

> When the Lord your God brings you into the land he swore to your fathers, to Abraham, Isaac and Jacob, to give you . . . then when you eat and are satisfied, *be careful that you do not forget the Lord*, who brought you out of Egypt, out of the land of slavery. (Deuteronomy 6.10–12, my italics)

Building on this covenant commission of faithfulness are the expected blessings for the people and the benefits to the land itself. Indeed this is one of the prominent themes developed throughout the Old Testament, that of the relationship between land and the faithful or unfaithful occupants. Faithfulness produces fruitfulness and good harvests; unfaithfulness results in famine and the blighting of the land.[1]

A more detailed reference to this principle is found in the instructions for the year of Jubilee, when the land would be rested from crop planting for one year. There were natural concerns, among a farming community, that this might be impractical and over-idealistic. As if in answer to this question the writer of Leviticus repeats the call to faithful covenant keeping:

> Follow my decrees and be careful to obey my laws, and you will live safely in the land. Then the land will yield its fruit, and you will eat your fill and live there in safety . . . I will send you such a blessing in the sixth year that the land will yield enough for three years. (Leviticus 25.18–21)

The blessing referred to here is the promise of abundant crop production, far in excess of the normal yield from the land. We should remind ourselves of course that the objective of this blessing is not that we can become formulaic or mechanistic in our endeavour to produce great profit to ourselves but that we live in harmony with God's ways and reap the blessings to be found there. The real goal is to live in the safe arms of God, who provides for our needs and our environment.

Blessings or curses?

This theme of covenant obedience and its outcomes is starkly presented in the form of choosing destiny, whether to be the people who are blessed because they keep God's laws or cursed because they have broken covenant with God. The content of the blessings for the new community of Israel in their land of promise ranges from having healthy children and livestock to good crop production, the defeat of all enemies and a holy living that will inspire all nations to recognize that God is among them (Deut. 28.1–14).

Sadly, disobedience to the covenant would bring curses tantamount to the destruction of the entire community and the ultimate disgrace of the loss of the land gifted by God (Deut. 28.15–68). It is therefore no small wonder that Joshua reminded the people of this on the eve of entering the land of promise, to ensure they would keep covenant (Josh. 8.34).

What is interesting is that the blessings and curses are presented as a choice. It is a reminder to choose wisely the path we intend to take in life. As my former Bible College principal, Stanley Banks, once said, 'By the grace of God you can choose not to sin but you cannot choose not to have the consequences of your sin.' In a very graphic way the community of Israel is commanded to stand atop two adjoining mountains once they secure their place in the promised land. From the summits of Mount Gerizim and Ebal, which face each other across the River Jordan, they are to declare respectively the blessings and curses of God as a powerful reminder to choose wisely.

It is not inappropriate for us today to learn from the principle of that action and declare aloud that we are going to be the faithful, covenant-keeping people of our Lord and saviour Jesus Christ and that we expect the blessings that he gives those who sincerely follow him. Neither is this declaration of blessings confined to the Old Testament. James, in his general letter to the churches, picks up this exhortation to keeping covenant and being blessed. He challenges Christians to stand apart from the moral degradation of their culture and society and become doers of the word of God. They will then be blessed in whatever they do (James 1.25).[2] The word of God for James would have been the Old Testament Scriptures, so here is an example of taking the principles of the old covenant and connecting them to the faithful followers of Jesus Christ. Consequently I believe that there is a precedent for the Christian church or community to declare its commitment to the new covenant of Jesus Christ and to living in obedience to the word of God for today. We should do this in full expectation that God will bless us with the gifts and abilities we need to be those faithful followers of his. Once again we remind ourselves that blessings are not to prosper us in our private ambitions but are designed to enable us to give God glory in the world that others may know that Jesus lives.

I am deeply impressed with the way the Methodist Church holds an annual covenant service in order to renew its commitment to Christ and the expectation that God will honour its faithfulness with the blessings of growth and successful evangelization. The Covenant Prayer itself is modelled on an earlier prayer of John Wesley:

I am no longer my own but yours.
Put me to what you will,
rank me with whom you will;
put me to doing,
  put me to suffering;
let me be employed for you
  or laid aside for you,
exalted for you
  or brought low for you;
let me be full,
  let me be empty,
let me have all things,
  let me have nothing;
I freely and wholeheartedly yield all things
to your pleasure and disposal.

And now, glorious and blessèd God,
Father, Son and Holy Spirit,
you are mine, and I am yours.
So be it.
And the covenant now made on earth,
let it be ratified in heaven. Amen.[3]

This is indeed a glorious prayer of personal devotion and commitment, and its focus is on individual service to God and the community. In my years of working for the renewal of churches in their life and commission I have found it helpful to encourage them to include a corporate way of praying for the renewing of the ministry of their church and to link this with the expectation of blessing. I have used various liturgies in which we have explored the story of the church in question and unpacked the various issues currently shaping it. There were factors that wounded the church and bent it out of shape, and the congregation has owned these through confession and repentance; there were factors that were good, and we equally owned these in celebration and honour. I have discovered that what we do not celebrate will shrink through lack of affirmation.

The final part of the event is to go publicly about all the places of ministry within the church building and anoint these with holy water, making the sign of the cross. I invite everyone to take part because it is tantamount to the Christian community, young and old, all owning the church and its life as their life. I encourage the people when they are anointing these foci of ministry – the pulpit, the choir stalls, the Holy Communion table and altar rail, the wardens' seats, the place where the minister sits or stands to lead services, the entrance to the building where warm welcome is to be given – to pray a simple prayer such as 'I anoint you with this holy water so that by the grace of God you come alive again and become the place where God's touch is given to all.'

When all this is done the congregation comes together as one and we pray a keeping-of-covenant prayer such as the following:

Today we renew our commitment to be the people of God in this town.
Today we dedicate this place and ourselves to be the Servant of God and at the service of our town.
Today we have decided to follow Jesus and to keep the word of God as our guide.

Today we have asked God to forgive our sins and to transform us again by the power of the Holy Spirit.
Today we have asked God to restore his love to us and through us to express that love to all without discrimination.
Today we start again in faithfulness and hope and therefore look to God to give us the blessings that will enable us to be the church he wants us to be.
O gracious God, open the windows of heaven and pour out your blessings on us so we will grow in faith and effective witness for you. Amen.

It has been my experience that God loves to honour actions and prayers like this. I well remember facilitating a coming together of church leaders at Wareham Priory some years ago. I was invited to lead this event by a small group of those leaders who felt that the life and witness of their churches in that area was stifled and blocked in some way. I gave some teaching in the morning on themes I have just outlined, and was just about to give another presentation when one of the church leaders asked if he could say a few words before I started. He stood in front of us all and declared that he was a new pastor in that town but had discovered that his church had a history of considering itself superior to other churches. On behalf of his church he apologized for its arrogance and asked the other church leaders to forgive him and his church for their attitude. This was a humble and powerful turning moment in that day as one leader after another responded in a similar fashion. The Holy Spirit moved among us to break down the differences and deadlock in church relationships shaping the Christian witness in that town and area.

We ended that cold, January day by gathering in a group at the front of the sanctuary and declaring before God that we were going to be the people of God who kept his covenant to love one another. There were outpourings of prayers for each others' churches as well as prayers for the well-being of the different communities from which we had come. The final prayer was that God would now bless us and make us a blessing. Out of that time of repentance and renewal has come a wonderful expression of Christian witness with the birth of the Connect Celebration Conferences, which over 1,000 people have attended. These are wonderful weekends of fellowship and teaching with vibrant worship. However, what stands out so strongly in these events is the tangible love and respect and celebration of each other that characterizes each event. It is no small wonder that so many people have come to faith in the Lord Jesus Christ when they experience this quality of caring among such a diverse community of people. Truly the prayers on that January afternoon to be blessed by God have been realized far beyond their expectations. Let us then take seriously the exhortation of James and become the people who ensure we are keeping the covenant of Christ and expecting the blessings of God on all we do for him.

Perhaps a final mention of this theme comes from the book of Malachi with which the Old Testament closes. Malachi conducted his prophetic challenges to Israel most likely during the restoration period after the return from exile, and possibly during the time of Ezra and Nehemiah. The book falls into six sections, each introduced with a question such as, 'You ask', followed by God's answer. The first three focus on the broken covenant, the final three on God's intervention to restore the covenant.

The fifth section focuses on a challenge to the people to stop defrauding God with cheap worship offerings and to bring all the proper tithes and offerings to the restored temple. Then comes the bold statement from God daring the people to test his generosity with their obedience.

> 'Bring the whole tithe into the storehouse, that there may be food in my house. Test me in this,' says the LORD Almighty, 'and see if I will not throw open the floodgates of heaven and pour out so much blessing that there will not be room enough to store it.' (Malachi 3.10)

Once again the content of the blessing is spelled out in familiar terms of crop abundance, freedom from pestilences that threaten the harvest and a recognition by the surrounding nations of the visible manifestation of God's favour on the land of the Israelites. Yoilah Yilpet is right to focus our attention on the context of repentance and obedience. He says that any challenge to test the Lord must be related to a call for repentance that demonstrates our faith and dependence on God. God promises an overabundance of his blessings if he is obeyed.[4]

What are we to make of this today? Its original application was to a community in chaos and far from honouring God. God set them a challenge to renew their obedience to his covenant, and promised mighty blessings if they did. Can we use this particular text and make a *general* use of it for our own lives? I think we can if we bear in mind that it is in the context of keeping covenant obedience and not some formula to get ourselves the blessings we want. The evidence from Scripture reveals that God has made general promises to bless those who honour and keep his covenant. We have seen that those blessings are not perks but gifts to establish and enhance our full dependency on God and to give him glory.

Living in unity

Perhaps one of the things God is most passionate about is when human beings learn to live in harmony – to celebrate rather than be threatened by differences – and when we serve the Lord in the unity of God's love and purpose. It is therefore no small wonder that when Jesus prayed his agonizing prayer in the garden of Gethsemane before his trial and crucifixion, he asked three times that his followers would live in unity (John 17.11, 20–23). He prayed for unity because it has a powerful purpose and effect. Jesus wanted his followers to be one because it reflected the oneness between the divine Father and Son and so demonstrated the fulfilling of God's will through the life of Jesus and also therefore through the united Church. The other purpose was that the unbelieving world would see and know through the unity of Jesus' disciples that God had demonstrated his high love for them in sending his son to be their saviour. Unity therefore is not a cosmetic sharing of policies and aspirations but a mighty resource for the power of God to change lives and to crack open the darkness of this world with the sight of the incredible love of God in Jesus Christ. No wonder Jesus was so insistent that he wrestled in prayer that we might obtain it.

The most striking reference to the power of unity is to be found in Psalm 133.

> Behold, how good and how pleasant it is
> For brothers to dwell together in unity!
> It is like the precious oil upon the head,
> Coming down upon the beard,
> Even Aaron's beard,

Coming down upon the edge of his robes.
It is like the dew of Hermon
Coming down upon the mountains of Zion;
For there the LORD commanded the blessing – life forever.

(NASB)

The last verse is really inspiring because it refers to the fact that God so loves and celebrates our unity that wherever he finds it he commands the blessings that suffuse our unity with the power of his endless life. What the psalmist also wants to demonstrate in keeping with the conclusion of this poem is the extravagance of the proportion of this blessing.

Two images of the blessing of unity are given in this psalm: the anointing of the high priest Aaron and the dew of Mount Hermon flowing down on to the hill of Zion and the city of Jerusalem. According to Donald Coggan, the background to the blessing was the gathering of worshippers from many different countries and widely different cultures, who nonetheless came with the common purpose to worship the God of Israel at festival time in Jerusalem. In this way they were a band of brothers.[5]

The first image of blessing focuses on the high priest, who would have functioned as the master of ceremonies at the feast this band of brothers had come to celebrate in the temple. Aaron is mentioned in particular because he was the archetypal and first high priest, and in many ways a special example of that role. The imagery of pouring the oil on Aaron's head comes from the original commissioning of Aaron and his sons to serve in the sacrifices at the temple of God. The original reference to this from the book of Exodus states that an amount of anointing oil over five stones in weight was prepared, and some of it was poured over the high priest's head (Exod. 30.22–30). This is the language and description of abundance and plenty. Keil and Delitzsch point out that only Aaron had oil poured over him, while his sons were merely anointed.[6] We are meant to be impressed with the extravagance of the oil used and see this as a reference to and encouragement of the generosity of blessing that God will pour out on those who live and work in unity together.

The second image is that of the dew of Mount Hermon, the highest mountain in the region. The three peaks that comprise Hermon are almost permanently snow-capped, and from its melting waters emerges the River Jordan. The dew is famous for bringing coolness and refreshment to this often dry and hot landscape. Incidentally, it houses the only ski resort in the state of Israel! So one of the pictures to emerge from this of how God blesses, is the range of those blessings' influence and their refreshing and life-giving qualities. But we can legitimately go further. In answer to the question, 'What is the dew of Hermon?' I heard a preacher say, 'Tons of snow!' He wanted us to imagine the effects of all that snow coming down on Mount Zion. It is an exaggeration of course, but it accurately reflects the note of extravagance that this psalm wants to paint about how God blesses the people who are united. After all, it repeatedly uses the term 'coming down' to describe the effects of unity and its accompanying blessings.

We have already noted how Jesus prayed passionately for unity among his followers. Cyril Okorocha says that it is therefore no surprise that the Apostle Paul emphasized the need for unity so much in his letters to the churches.[7] Paul was no stranger to the powers that could tear a church apart, and he constantly encouraged churches to keep hold of the unity of the faith (Eph. 4.3). He returned to this theme again and again (cf. 2 Cor. 13.11; Eph. 4.1–6; Phil. 2.2–8; Col. 3.14–15). Okorocha goes on to say that perhaps one of the greatest needs for the people of God today is to recover the ministry of reconciliation.[8] We would do well to learn again from Jesus' words on making reconciliation a priority, even if it means putting down our cherished gifts (Matt. 5.23–24). This came home very forcibly to me when I was the incumbent of a church in Leicestershire. I had only been the rector for a short while, and the church was struggling to move forward in its life. It was the familiar story of finding change difficult and tending to cling to the past and keep their distance from newcomers with new ideas.

The church already had a monthly healing service but it was more tolerated than welcomed. Consequently I suggested that we move the healing service from the Sunday evening to a Saturday night and that we make it ecumenical. The very first service was poorly attended by my own congregation and there were only about 20 people from the other churches in the town. Just before I announced the opening hymn, my verger interrupted me, saying that he was not happy with what was happening and that it was not a proper Church of England service! When I pointed out that it was an ecumenical service he did not seem to be impressed, going on to say that he wasn't at all sure why he had come to this service. After struggling within himself he blurted out that he hated his younger brother. Apparently his mother had died and his father remarried. The younger brother was born and all his father's love seemed to be poured out over that son and he felt left out. It caused him to resent his brother. 'The only good thing about him', he went on to say, 'is that he lives far away in South Africa. And when he comes home we go through this pretence of being good Christian brothers.'

As we were all gripped by the verger's story, we did not notice the late arrivals sliding quietly into church. Suddenly one of them jumped to his feet and shouted out the verger's name. It was his brother and he had come home! The verger was surprised and shocked because his younger brother had doubtless heard him telling everyone in the room that he had nursed a resentment towards him for many years. 'Why have you come home now?' he asked. What followed was truly amazing. The younger brother told his sibling that he had always known that he hated him, and why, so he resolved to do something about it. He decided to leave home and get out of the way so that the older brother could have their father's love to himself. But sadly this didn't work out as hoped. The younger brother had become a school teacher and had been offered promotion to the headship of a school, and as he was writing his acceptance letter a thought occurred to him. He had not really prayed and sought guidance over this appointment, so he absentmindedly opened his desktop calendar of Bible verses to see what the Scripture for the day was. It read, 'If you are offering your gift at the altar and there remember that your brother or sister has something against you, leave your gift there in front of the altar. First go and be reconciled to them' (Matt. 5.23–24).

This young man asked for permission to delay his response to the offer and was refused. 'So I declined the promotion,' he said, 'and thought I should come home to you so we could be reconciled.' The enormity of what he had given up and why hit the older brother with great power, and after a brief hesitation the two brothers ran to each other across that church and in a flood of emotion embraced and were reconciled.

I was suddenly aware of great power in that church. All of us were deeply touched by the love of God. I can confidently say that this reconciliation story affected the whole church and other churches in that town, and out of it grew a tremendous willingness to work together in a way we never had before. I think we are long overdue in recognizing the importance of the ministry of reconciliation and the unity that is its goal. Indeed Scripture says that we have an ambassadorial commission to be reconcilers (2 Cor. 5.18–20). It was Monsignor Michael Buckley, the founder of El Shaddai Ministries, who said that reconciliation is the most radical form of healing. I think that the blessings commanded for moments of reconciliation can transform our churches and communities.

A final example of this I would like to share comes from taking part in a conference in Uganda in January 2013 that was ostensibly to launch the African Chapter of the International Ecumenical Fellowship. The title of the conference was 'Healing Wounded History', attended by the Roman Catholic and Anglican Archbishops, a host of Bishops and church leaders from various denominations, two Muslim Sheikhs, the President of the B'hai faith of Uganda and many international delegates. I was asked to give two keynote addresses on the theme of the conference, following which a number of scholarly papers would be presented on related themes, politically, spiritually and economically. Right from the outset there was a real sense of the presence and blessing of God on our gathering – we were serious about living in unity and respecting difference. I gave my first keynote address and then sat down and awaited the first of the scholarly papers. One by one the presenters said that they had never been to a scholarly conference like this one where God had shown up!

Then they chose to open their hearts and share the long, unhealed pain of having lived through genocide in Uganda, watching helplessly while their families and friends had been killed by some of the groups represented by people at the conference. They had mostly been children when these things had happened, but they had stored them up in their hearts. However, on that day they were opening up to God and each other and laying down their pain at the foot of the cross. They wanted to be part of the healing of their land and they wanted to do it with each other. There were apologies between Christians and between tribal groups. There were apologies to the Muslims for not helping them in time of famine, and a determination to go to their villages to translate their apologies into serious acts of caring. I was overwhelmed by the courage of those who opened up long-held wounds, and blessed to see how God began to heal and reconcile and bring us all to a place of new expectation of what he was doing among us.

When we find unity we will experience the blessings that God gives to make our unity a resource for healing and transformation in our world. God will command blessings because he is so eager for unity to grow, reflecting the heart of our heavenly Father and his son Jesus Christ.

Holy living

One of my favourite movies is *It's A Wonderful Life*, in which James Stewart plays George Bailey, a man fed up with life who in a moment of despair wishes he had never been born. He even contemplates suicide by jumping into an ice-cold river in full winter flood. Yet George has a guardian angel who grants his request never to have been born, though George does not at first realize it. So when George decides to go back home he finds everything has changed dramatically. His younger brother whom he saved from drowning in a pond when he was six years was never rescued and so died – because George had never been born. That same brother had in fact grown up and during the Second World War had saved the lives of thousands on a troopship – but because George had never been born, the men perished. George's eccentric uncle had been put in an asylum because George wasn't there to watch over him. The town had even changed its name because George had been not there to combat the greedy and dark heart of Mr Potter, who long had designs on owning everything and everyone.

What George is privileged to see, though painfully, is the change in his community without his having been born to make his own contribution to its shape. He saw a town without the blessings he had been born to give, and this leads to the film's punchline: 'You see, George, you had a wonderful life!'

It is the same theme that the compiler of the book of Proverbs wishes to make in his unique compare-and-contrast style.

> Through the blessing of the upright a city is exalted,
> but by the mouth of the wicked it is destroyed. (Proverbs 11.11)

> Blessings crown the head of the righteous,
> but violence overwhelms the mouth of the wicked.
> The name of the righteous is used in blessings,
> but the name of the wicked will rot. (Proverbs 10.6–7)

> Whoever says to the guilty, 'You are innocent',
> will be cursed by peoples and denounced by nations.
> But it will go well with those who convict the guilty,
> and rich blessing will come on them. (Proverbs 24.24–25)

People who live holy lives make a difference for the better for others in their communities. They are like salt preserving the good and light shining in the dark. In many ways these passages show that the individuals are themselves a blessing to their community. The blessings that God gives them seem to amount to becoming a major resource for the good of others. As we aspire to live holy lives it is perfectly acceptable to pray that God pours out blessings on our lives so that we become a force for the good of others. It is also a good thing that we bless such people with the blessings that will enhance their witness and effect in the community.

So for a policeman we could pronounce:

> God bless you with an increase of justice and fairness in all your dealings with others. The Lord give you the strength to do the right thing and protect you as you care for the vulnerable. God bless your life with a love for all people no matter what their colour, race or sex.

For a doctor or nurse we could pronounce:

> God bless your skill as you look after the needs of those who are sick or ill. The Lord bless you as you come alongside those in distress and help you to listen well. The Lord make his healing touch pass through you to meet others at their point of need.

For a father or mother we could pronounce:

> God bless you and make you a great father/mother to your children. The Lord give you an increase in your ability to nurture your children and support them as they grow. The Lord empower you to love your children and be the one to encourage them, to recognize their gifts and celebrate them.

You could possibly think of others, and if so I challenge you to pray and pronounce your blessing prayers with them and for them. Doing this also helps to remind us that holy living is not just a private devotional path where we get closer to God and become further removed from community. The essential core of holy living is to live as much like Jesus as we can for the benefit of our communities. Holiness is not therefore an otherworldly pursuit but very much a quality of good living pursued in and for this world.

It is this that lies behind the great lament of Jesus over the city of Jerusalem: 'Jerusalem, Jerusalem, you who kill the prophets and stone those sent to you, how often I have longed to gather your children together, as a hen gathers her chicks under her wings, but you were not willing' (Luke 13.34). He undoubtedly touched for the better the lives of many who lived in that city, but he longed to reach even more. It challenges me to call down the blessings of God on all those who try their best to live holy lives in their towns and cities, so that together we become more effective in transforming the places where we live.

Saving grace

The final thread of expecting blessing because we live in the place to be blessed lies in the very act of experiencing the saving graces of God. This can first be identified by another thread running throughout the Old Testament, which is that Israel's purpose lies beyond its own boundaries. It is to be a light to the nations. In being redeemed and rescued and given a land of promise to live in, so Israel is to bless other nations with the same connection and knowledge of Yahweh (cf. Isa. 2.2–5). Over and over again the emphasis is on the fact that it is redeemed Israel that is to be a blessing to other nations (Isa. 44.3; Zech. 8.13).

Paul picks up this theme when he writes to the Galatian church and tells them the salvation they rejoice in is in fact the intended blessing of Abraham (Gal. 3.8,14; cf. Acts 3.25). He draws out that the content of the blessing made possible through Abraham is the gift of the Holy Spirit.

Over and over again there is reference to the blessings of the good news itself, at the heart of which is the restored and saving relationship with God through Jesus and the life in the Spirit of God. We become indeed a new creation through this blessing. In writing to the church in Rome, Paul reminds them that God blesses all who call on the Lord (Rom. 10.12). In planning to visit this church he states boldly that he intends to come in the full measure of the blessing of Christ (Rom. 15.29; cf. 1 Cor. 9.23). Finally blessing is seen as a consummation to be eagerly awaited, namely the return of Jesus Christ to this planet to rule and reign in righteousness (Titus 2.13).

While not undermining the power and importance of the good news as blessing, we need to distinguish that here we have references to the primary blessing of knowing the saving love of God and all its benefits. Alongside this are the specific blessings we are examining throughout this book. Yet both kinds of blessing are to be actively sought and not passively awaited. If we belong to Christ then it is perfectly reasonable that we ask and expect God to bless us with the ongoing benefits of being his redeemed people. Surely this lies behind our confidence to expect God to deepen our knowledge and intimacy with him and to give us the blessing of the Holy Spirit? We can cry out that he bless us powerfully with those gifts and graces we need to become more like the people he wants us to be. As we shall see in the next chapter, we do indeed need to dare to cry out to God to bless us if we are going to live out the good news life he has bought for us with the high price of the death of his son Jesus.

Praise God, from whom all blessings flow!
Praise him, all creatures here below!
Praise him above, ye heavenly host!
Praise Father, Son and Holy Ghost! (Thomas Ken)[9]

6

Wrestling for blessing

'Oh, that you would bless me!' (1 Chronicles 4.10)

The Old Testament contains two remarkable stories of individuals whose very survival hinged on their getting the blessing they so longed for. They are Jacob and Jabez. There are a number of parallels in their stories: both have difficult births; both have significant names that connect them to the need to be blessed; both are going through desperate circumstances; both demand to be blessed; and both receive that blessing.

As we explore their stories we will raise the question, 'Is it right for us today to ask for or even demand a blessing from God?'

A difficult birth

Jacob's birth is an answer to prayer. His mother, Rebekah, was failing to conceive but in answer to Isaac's prayer she becomes pregnant to twin boys. However, there is a desperate struggle in Rebekah's womb as the twin boys fight for supremacy. David H. Stern translates this passage from Genesis 25.22 as, 'The children fought with each other inside her so much that she said, "If it's going to be like this, why go on living?"'[1] The Hebrew word used here means 'to crush', and it graphically describes the aggression and hostility that was going to determine the relationship between the brothers for the whole of their lives.[2] Gottfried Fitzer points out that the particular form of the Greek word found in the Septuagint version of this account can refer to ill-treatment. Fitzer quotes its use in the Wisdom of Solomon 17.18, where it describes stampeding animals. In so doing he describes a prenatal struggle in the battle to be born first and so rule the other.[3] Small wonder Rebekah despaired of her life, that the pain drove her to prayer and to ask God what was going wrong with her pregnancy.

The story of Jabez's cry for blessing comes almost as a surprise and a relief within a long list of the clans and tribes of Israel (1 Chron. 4.9–10). He suddenly appears and as promptly disappears from the pages of Scripture. We are told of the testimony of his unnamed mother that Jabez was born in pain. The Hebrew word for pain used here can mean hardship and distress and refer to emotional and mental as well as physical suffering.[4] Consequently, though we are not given the details we can conclude that this traumatic birth deeply affected mother and child and left a lasting legacy. It would not be the first time an adult lived out or transcended the legacies of his or her birth.[5] Whatever the effects on Jabez, it drove him to seek a change of destiny through blessing. The account also mentions that he was more honourable than his brothers, but again the details are missing. He could not have been more different from Jacob in this respect, who seems to have made it his career to outwit his older brother to gain ascendency – there was no honour in this.

Significant names

The name Jacob means heel-holder and refers both to the startling fact that at his birth he was grabbing hold of his older brother as he emerged from the womb and also to his lifelong propensity to use his wits to get his own way. In their commentary on Genesis Keil and Delitzsch compare this birth move of Jacob to wrestling, where an attempt is made to throw the opponent by grasping his heel.[6] Jacob's chief target for his wrestling hold was of course Esau, and we read of how in time he used his brother's hunger to get him to sell his birthright (Gen. 25.29–34). The birthright in patriarchal times embraced the chieftainship, the rule over the brethren and the entire family and the title to the blessing of the promise that included the future possession of Canaan and of covenant fellowship with Jehovah.[7] It is interesting to note that despite getting the birthright blessing from Isaac, he nonetheless needed and wanted God to bless him. As we shall soon see, this would be for a very different purpose.

Jabez is also named from his birth experience, his name (*jbz*) means 'pain', so we have a play on this word because his heart's desire is to be blessed so as not to experience pain (*jzb* – in Hebrew these are similar sounding words). Jabez evidently thought that his name expressed his destiny and so wanted God to reverse his situation – the stimulus and starting point of his prayer.[8] He seeks blessing for very personal reasons: he wants to be delivered from evil but more importantly from extreme pain in his life that was signalled by the mode of his birth and seems to have haunted him ever since. However, unlike Jacob his difficult birth did not end in bitter rivalry with his siblings. While we might want to think that his request for a blessing that delivers him from pain is a selfish one, it is perfectly understandable and describes half the prayer requests in the Bible if not the majority of all the intercessions of the faithful!

Desperate circumstances

Things could not have been worse for Jacob. He is once again a refugee with nowhere to live, even though he had outwitted his greedy uncle Laban and was heavily laden with cattle and servants and an extended family. He is returning home not knowing what he is to face, but he can't take his mind off that memory of 20 years ago when he dispossessed his brother Esau of his birthright. He resorts to his default position of scheming and outwitting and sends on ahead to his brother various gifts and servants, who are given instructions on precisely what to say (Gen. 32.3–5). However, some of the servants return to tell Jacob that his brother is coming to greet him, but bringing with him 400 men (Gen. 32.6)! You can forgive Jacob for panicking and concluding that this is not a good sign. So he now lavishly piles on the gifts and the grovelling speeches through his servant. All the gifts and the words are intended to impress Esau and persuade him to drop any grudges he may have in his heart towards Jacob. The final act sees Jacob send on ahead his whole family, and for the first time in 20 years he is once again alone and without any bargaining chips to outwit his opponent. It is at this moment of powerlessness that God pounces on Jacob in a wrestling match.

For Jabez the dark shadow that looms over his life is the strong desire to be kept from harm. J. Barton Page says that the word used here for 'harm' is a general term with wide coverage. It can refer to what tastes nasty right through to intrinsic moral and spiritual evil.[9] So was Jabez fighting with his brothers who sought to harm him? Was he under siege to protect his land from those who would seize it from him? Was he struggling with temptations beyond his ability to resist? We are simply not told and must therefore conclude from the desperate longing in his heart to be blessed that his struggle was serious and possibly life threatening.

Many commentators see a link here with the words 'Lead us not into temptation but deliver us from the evil one', which is found in the prayer that Jesus has taught us (Matt. 6.13). Bruce Wilkinson offers a radical commentary on Jabez's desire to be kept from harm. He suggests that what is meant here is that we learn like Jabez simply to stay out of the arena of battling with evil.[10] What he is trying to point out is that far too often we pray for help to endure the temptations and overcome them. While there is a time and a place for this, Wilkinson suggests that in addition we must learn to pray for those times when we are kept right out of the battle. I am reminded of an illustration of this that I heard from an old Gospel preacher when I was young.

> A rich man lived at the top of a mountain and the only way to reach his castle was by way of a narrow road that wound itself around and up to the top. One day it was advertised that he needed a new carriage driver because his usual driver had retired. Three men arrived to be interviewed for the job. 'How good a driver are you?' the rich man asked the first. 'Well,' said the driver, 'I can take you within 12 inches of the cliff edge on your mountain road and you will be safe with me.' The rich man asked the same question of the second driver, who replied, 'I can take you within six inches of the cliff edge on your mountain road and you will be safe with me.' Finally he asked the same question of the third driver, who replied, 'I would stay as far away from the cliff edge on your mountain road as possible and you will be safe with me.' To which do you think he gave the job? The one who stayed as far from that tempting cliff edge as possible!

I think there is a definite place when we do need to ask God to protect us both in the heat of battle and from battles and temptations that we cannot nor should handle. Scripture has many examples of those who sought escape from various battles. Paul described a condition he struggled with as a thorn in the flesh and messenger of Satan to torment him (2 Cor. 12.7). Even though he prayed to be freed from it, God said no. This was one battle he would have to face and it would become the primary place in his life where grace made up for his weaknesses. I think a parallel episode is that of Jesus praying in the garden of Gethsemane, where he asked that he might escape the battle of suffering that awaited him (Matt. 26.39). Yet he also added that his primary wish was to do the Father's will rather than his own, and so he entered into his last battle of crucifixion and death. However, Jesus' prayer in Gethsemane did focus on asking the Father to protect his disciples from the evil one (John 17.15). So it seems that we need to discern those times when we need strength and protection for the fight and those when we are kept from needless warfare.

Jabez wanted the blessing of God to deliver him from evil and prevent him from being deeply harmed. It was a critical issue in his life and he was prepared to cry out to God for the blessing that brought deliverance. Bruce Wilkinson offers a useful prayer for those moments when we need to be aware of the battles we face and those we should avoid:

> Lord, keep me safe from the pain and grief that sin brings. For the dangers that I can't see, or the ones that I think I can risk because of my experience, put up a supernatural barrier. Protect me, Father, by your power! Amen.[11]

A demand to be blessed

The graphic picture of Jacob wrestling with an angel is perhaps one of the most memorable accounts in Scripture. It is a desperate fight for Jacob because whatever he hoped to gain from this struggle he looked certain to fail. Opinions differ as to whom he thought he was wrestling. It began in the dark and so he could not see the face of his opponent. Perhaps he thought it was Esau or one of his henchmen. However, as daybreak dawned Jacob shockingly realized that it was God himself he was wrestling. This seems to be backed up by his later confession when he named the spot Peniel, which means face of God. Something dramatically changed in Jacob at this moment. Despite all the visions, dreams and promises from God that he would inherit the blessings of Abraham, he nonetheless resorted to his usual outwitting to try and get his own way. He just could not rest in blessing, he had to try and grab it! But when he realized it was God he was fighting he held on to the Lord for a very different reason. According to Phil Moore, Jacob's confession at this point could have been:

> *I've spent my whole life wrestling with you*, he effectively confesses, *when all along you chose me while I was still inside my mother's womb! I've no hope left in this world outside of your blessing, and if you won't give it to me purely by your grace then I might as well die as try to make it all begin with me.*[12]

Jacob's wrestling match illustrates a change in relationship to blessing. Now it was time for him to learn how to rest in blessing instead of trying to use his own ingenuity and scheming to get it. Consequently his deep cry of 'I will not let you go unless you bless me' (Gen. 32.26) is not so much a demand on God as a mark of his deep need to live in God's blessing.

Jabez's request for blessing is simple and direct: 'Oh, that you would bless me' (1 Chron. 4.10). Charles Haddon Spurgeon wrote that the very substance of this prayer seems to lie in the intensity of the request.[13] In other words there is a lot of meaning riding on that 'Oh'. It can be interpreted to mean 'I really wish' or 'If you do, I will'. This is the language of bargaining, but as none appears in the prayer we can safely assume this is a deep heart's cry for blessing. The emphasis on longing for help is underlined by the version of this text in the Septuagint, the Greek Old Testament, which uses the reference to blessing twice. It could be translated as 'In blessing you will have blessed.' Most translations insert 'indeed' to emphasize the depth of feeling in the request to be blessed. This is no casual or passive request but a make-or-break cry of the heart.

Whereas Jacob does not specify the content of the blessing he so wanted, Jabez is very clear about the issues he wanted his blessing to touch and transform. They are:

1 to enlarge his borders;
2 to have the hand of God on his life;
3 to be kept from harm and pain.

It is important not to see these three as extra to his blessing; they are rather the shape and content of the blessing he requires and needs. They are personal to Jabez's life and circumstances and he wants the blessing to be more than just a pat on the back for being a faithful believer. Neither must we separate the blessing that speaks of personal relationship from the content of that blessing. William E. Arp says that the emphasis of all blessings is on relationship-building between God and the recipient of his blessing and favour.[14] He cites the words of Deuteronomy in support. In faithfully keeping the covenant relationship the community of Israel will be blessed by an increase in the population, in the crops of the fields and cattle. 'You will be blessed more than any other people; none of your men or women will be childless, nor will any of your livestock be without young. The LORD will keep you free from every disease' (Deut. 7.12–15).[15]

John Hartley takes this further in respect of the final outcome of Job's restoration from a hideous sickness when he says, 'The emphasis is not so much on rewards as on the visible evidence of Yahweh's favour bestowed anew on Job.'[16] As we have already outlined in this book, we need to keep in creative connection that blessings are about enjoying the favour of God and in tangible form.

Jabez had personal needs and he wanted God's blessing to meet those needs.

Enlarge my borders

It is generally agreed that this section of 1 Chronicles reflects the return from exile when everything was insecure. Jabez's request can be seen as a straightforward one for more land, which would increase security and prosperity. We can be forgiven for asking if this is a form of prosperity doctrine! It does lead to a second question: 'Is it right to ask God for more and if so to what purpose?'

Bruce Wilkinson says that Jabez's request was much more than a desire for more real estate. He suggests that he wanted more influence, more responsibility and more opportunity to make a mark for the God of Israel.[17] From here he develops a direct link between Jabez's request and asking God to enable us to move beyond the borders of our limitations and take new territories of influence in Christian ministry. In fact he heralds the prayer of Jabez as being the very prayer we should all be regularly praying so that our sphere of ministry increases dramatically and many more people come to a saving knowledge of Jesus Christ in their lives. Among the many memorable stories in his book, Wilkinson tells that of Warren and his friend Dave. They had specifically prayed that God would bless them with the opportunity to witness to the Governor of

California that very weekend. In a letter to Wilkinson they wrote what happened next:

> By Sunday night when we got back from Sacramento, this is what happened. We had expressed our faith to two gas station attendants, four security guards, the head of the U.S. National Guard, the Director of the Department of Health, Education and Welfare for the State of California, the Head of the California Highway Patrol, the Governor's secretary, and finally the Governor himself.[18]

However, much as we applaud the sincere desire to reach as many people as possible with the good news of God's love for them, it has to be said that you cannot justify that from the prayer of Jabez. This prayer cannot handle the freight that Wilkinson puts on it and there is no history within Scripture that Jabez's prayer was ever used in this formulaic sense, nor is it even mentioned apart from its brief appearance in 1 Chronicles.

I am sure Jabez wanted to enlarge his lands so he could support his family better. So we do have to take seriously the whole issue of why we want a particular blessing and what purpose it will serve. I think Wilkinson does us a huge favour in this respect because we can only confidently call out to be blessed if its purpose will honour God and his will for our lives. I think this is what separates the request from being selfish gain and cheap prosperity to being something that serves the purposes of God for us. Wanting to be blessed is not the problem, it is why. Compare for example the desire and determination of Caleb to be given a certain mountain and pastures in which his family could live (Josh. 14.12–14), and the archetypal man Jesus mentions who built himself bigger barns so he could increase his prosperity but loses his own soul in the process (Luke 12.13–21). Caleb is blessed with gaining his desire because we are told that he wholeheartedly followed God. The rich man is judged because his purpose for gain is to store things up for himself to the exclusion of the needs of everyone else. Consequently the purpose for wanting what we want is important and must reflect that our hearts are first set on being wholeheartedly for God and his purposes in our lives. I think this is what lies behind the very injunction of Jesus for us to ask, seek and knock continuously until we obtain what is good for us and for his purposes in our lives (Matt. 7.7–8).

The hand of God on my life

When you consider that the vast majority of blessings in the Bible were conveyed through touch or the laying on of hands, this cry of Jabez seems to be the deep heart's request that the blessings never stop coming. The hand of God on a person's life denotes the presence of God to give support and a transformation of circumstances. The following are just a few examples:

- Ezra is safely conducted to the ruined city of Jerusalem to help rebuild the broken community of faith returned after 70 years of exile (Ezra 7.9).
- God's hand is on the person who wants to keep his rulings (Ps. 119.173).
- To have God's hand on your life is to be guided and strengthened in your walk of faith (Ps. 139.10).
- God's hand is on those who endeavour to live holy lives and who want to give his light to others (Isa. 42.6).
- God's hand was with the infant and persecuted church to the effect that many others came to a living faith in Jesus (Acts 11.21).

Consequently having the hand of God on your life denotes a continued dependency on God. This of course is no guarantee that life gets easier but it does mean it stays focused on God and God's will. When God laid his hand on Jacob when he was crying for blessing, it was to make him a semi-cripple who would need to lean on a staff for the rest of his life. Yet this semi-cripple would be a man of heavenly influence and power, demonstrated in his old age when we are told that he blessed Pharaoh and his sons while leaning on that staff (Gen. 47.7; Heb. 11.21). A similar situation is that of the Apostle Paul, on whom the Lord laid his hand and in the process gave him a thorn in the flesh that became a focus of awareness of the spiritual battles assailing his life and mission (2 Cor. 12.7ff.). However, although it remained with Paul for the rest of his life it also became the touchstone through which he learnt to depend on God for grace rather than rely on his abilities or possessions.

Keep me from harm and pain

We explored this part of Jabez's prayer earlier in this chapter, and have seen that this is not just a request for an easy and problem-free life. It is a request to be kept from evil and those battles we are not yet ready to fight.

Receiving the blessing

In order for Jacob to receive the blessing he was asked to confess his name and therefore nature. This time there is no prevarication – he owns up to having tried to get through life by scheming. Consequently the form and content of the blessing Jacob receives is a name and nature change. He is now to be called Israel, which means 'prevails with God'. Phil Moore says that Jacob is transformed from a heel grabber to a grace grabber.[19] Yet what a paradox is presented at the conclusion of the contest between God and Jacob as we take another look at the now blessed man. He has seen the face of God and lived, and is now a man with princely connections with the Almighty as he limps his way into power and destiny (Gen. 32.30–31)! He was not free from the tragedies that would follow on from this moment (to see his daughter ravaged and his favourite son given up for dead), but all through these trials he would be the man who depended on God and ultimately triumphed against all the odds. He would end his days blessing and prophesying over his children and grandchildren.

With regard to Jabez we are simply told that God gave him the blessing he was looking for. God gave him what his heart desired because his life pleased God.

So in comparing and contrasting the blessing seekers, Jacob and Jabez, we return to our question, 'Is it right to ask God for specific blessings?' I think the answer is a clear 'Yes'. However, blessings are not given lightly or without purpose. To obtain them we need to be clear what it is we are asking God to grant us, and to assure ourselves that the request flows out of fellowship with God and will enhance his purposes in our lives.

Asking for God's blessing on your life

The following are some suggestions for a process by which we seek and find the blessings God will give us.

Examine your heart

- Why do I want this specific blessing? Are my motives selfish or is there some good reason and, if so, what is it?

- Is there anything I need to offer God in the way of confession? Jacob owned up to the way he had mismanaged his life, gifts and ministry calling. This could be an opportunity to give up your inappropriate habits and ways of living and recommit your life to the Lord and his calling on your life.

Decide on the blessing you need

A good way of focusing on the blessing you need is to complete sentences like the following:

- I want God to give me the blessing of . . .
- At this time in my life I need the blessing of . . .
- Dear God, bless me with . . .

What are the specific ingredients of that blessing?

Now take a moment to reflect on how you want this blessing fleshed out or filled in by God. For example, if you want God to bless your family life then you may want to ask specifically for:

- a flourishing of the gifts and graces you share with your husband or wife;
- growth in mutual celebration and honouring between parents and children;
- that your children will do well at university and continue to grow their faith in Christ;
- that God will remove all sicknesses and grant health and energy in which we can serve the Lord and the needs of our community;
- can you think of others?

This is an important part of asking for blessing so don't rush it! Write down and turn over in your heart the particular things you need God to do for you in blessing.

Ask the Holy Spirit to help you seek that blessing

It is always a good thing to ask the Spirit of God to bring life to all our prayers and quests of God precisely so that the Spirit may sift our hearts and encourage us when we are on the right track and redirect us when on the wrong. This is fully in keeping with those exhortations that Paul gave in his letter to the Roman church when he said that the Spirit intercedes for us and helps us to pray on target (Rom. 8.26–27).

Ask from the bottom of your heart

We cannot ask for blessings lightly. Unlike some intercessory prayers, blessings are a matter of life and death in comparison. We are seeking them because we need them and are convinced they will enable us to walk in that newness of life that is God's wish for us all.

There is also that need in the context of blessing in which we truly should know our utter dependence on the grace of God if our lives are going to have substance and meaning.

Surrender the blessings received to the purposes of God

When God's blessings begin to show up in our lives, this is our moment not only to thank God and give praise but also to commit such blessings to his deeper purposes.

Bearing in mind that blessings are intended to deepen and enhance our relationship with God, our prayer should be that this is precisely what receiving the blessing will achieve.

Let us close this chapter with a prayer:

> Oh God, I so want you to bless me. Bless me with health in my body so I can live well and long. Bless me with renewal in my spirit so I can serve you well. Bless me with a generous heart so I can take care of my family and love my children well. Amen.

7

The father's blessing

My father! Can't you also bless me?

(Genesis 27.34 *The Message*)

Some years ago I served as a chaplain for a holiday company called Mastersun on the Greek island of Kos. Everyone who attended was a Christian except for one young man in his twenties. His mother had brought him and I think he came against his better judgement! She took me aside at the beginning of the week and told me that she had brought her son to be saved and that I was to use every opportunity to tell him of his need. At various times throughout that holiday she would remind me of my duties to evangelize. To be honest, I didn't. I thought he looked harassed enough being in company that he found awkward, and he stayed on the fringes avoiding conversation.

However, there came a moment when I strolled into the bar and found him all alone, propped up against the counter having a quiet drink. He seemed to sense that I might use this moment to challenge him about his need of conversion and so turned to face me and said, 'OK then. It's just you and me. So give it your best shot!'

At that very moment his mother appeared in the doorway and saw us standing there. She looked at me with great expectation in her eyes and was encouraging me to seize the moment. As I stood there I thought about what I should say to him. Flashing through my mind came a picture of my own son, Joel, who was of a similar age. I asked myself, 'If it was my son standing here, what would I want to say to him?' I knew immediately and so I turned to him and said, 'You remind me so much of my son and I want to say to you what I would say to him.' He tensed up and replied, 'So what's that then?' I told him, 'You're a lovely boy! I bless you with being a lovely boy!'

He looked astonished. 'I've never been told that before', he said. His mother was not happy at all and said, 'That's not what I want you to tell him. Tell him he needs to be saved.' I turned to her in surprise and some anger: 'Surely you've been told by your father or mother that you're a lovely girl and that it blessed you?' Her silence and discomfort told me she hadn't.

I can't give you a wonderful conclusion and say this young man came to Jesus that day. I truly hope he received the blessing and that it helped him step into the truth of what God had called him to be. I can say that at the end of the holiday he took me aside, embraced me and thanked me for what I had said and for not pressurizing him. He added that he had recovered some joy in his heart.

It was a forceful reminder to me that there are so many children in the world who have never received the blessings only parents can give their children. Aaron Fruh is a conference speaker who specializes in teaching parents to bless their children verbally. He underlines how we live in a society that has embraced the culture of silence and how so many of us pass through childhood to adulthood and even old age without ever receiving a spoken blessing. Consequently he began to end his conferences by inviting men and women to come forward to receive a spoken blessing into their lives. He was overwhelmed when as many as 500 came forward to receive such a blessing, waiting in queues for over three hours to hear the simple words of blessing spoken over them.[1]

The father's blessing: a rhythm within Scripture

Noah

The Old Testament contains a strong thread of fathers blessing their sons. The first father's blessing in the Bible occurs when Noah blesses his two sons Shem and Japheth. On awaking from his drunken sleep and learning how these two sons had covered his nakedness with respect, he blessed them with growth and prosperity. He also cursed his other son Canaan for his disrespect (Gen. 9.26–27). Subsequent history was to prove that these blessings were no empty promises but carried the prophetic enabling of God.

Abraham

There is no direct record of Abraham blessing either of his sons, Ishmael and Isaac, but the blessing spoken by God over Abraham was that he would be a blessing to his family and that because of this they would go on to be a blessing to the nations. The first blessing from God states: 'I will make you into a great nation, and I will bless you; I will make your name great, and you will be a blessing' (Gen. 12.2). This was enough for Abraham to take the great risk of leaving his homeland and journeying out into the unknown – an amazing act of faith and obedience. The promise of being a blessing transformed the way he lived and shaped his expectations. The second reference to this blessing specifically involves the children yet to be born to him:

> Abraham will surely become a great and powerful nation, and all nations on earth will be blessed through him. For I have chosen him, so that he will direct his children and his household after him to keep the way of the Lord by doing what is right and just, so that the Lord will bring about for Abraham what he has promised him. (Genesis 18.18–19)

Although we are not seeing specific references to Abraham laying hands on his sons and pronouncing blessings, we are learning that in being a blessing we bring God's beneficial influence to others. The third blessing reference to Abraham makes this even more explicit: 'through your offspring all nations on earth will be blessed' (Gen. 22.18). Sylvia Gunter and Arthur Burk, in their book *Blessing your Spirit*, affirm this intention when they state, 'The blessings of the father are designed to gift a person's spirit with the Father's heart.'[2] We could almost say that the mission statement of the nation of Israel was to carry the blessings of Abraham's fidelity to God to the surrounding nations. They were not to dominate but to bless nations to achieve the God-given destiny he has set in the DNA of every nation and tribe. The blessings given to children are not to be hoarded but given away, so that others too may grow. Brian McLaren sees the blessing of Abraham as the tough love of God showing how the true greatness of blessing was not in domination but empowering.

> Abraham's identity is not greatness exploiting others (domination), greatness overthrowing others (revolution), greatness absorbing others (assimilation), greatness excluding others (purification), greatness resenting others (victimisation), greatness separated from others (isolation) or greatness at the expense of others (competition).[3]

Abraham's and his sons' greatness was for the sake of others, 'all peoples on earth will be blessed through you' (Gen. 12.3). It is a sad fact of history that Israel lost the blessings with their intentions and as a result lost their own national identity for almost two millennia. I am grateful for the writings of Bishop Tom Wright, who consistently reminds us that Jesus the Messiah came to complete what the sons of Abraham had failed to do. Jesus' whole mission was to be the blessed son bringing to the nations of the world the blessings of not only Father Abraham but of Father God. We should not be surprised, therefore, that he referred to God as Father so many times in his teachings – the word occurs almost 250 times in the New Testament.

Isaac

There is no mention of Isaac blessing his two sons until he is old and infirm and almost blind and ready to die. Consequently these blessings are heavily freighted with the issue of succession and importance. It was the normal understanding that the elder son would inherit all or the bulk of his father's estate. In other words there was a lot at stake for Jacob and Esau. This story from Genesis has already painted a picture of parental favouritism resulting in sibling rivalry, and the background to the moment of blessing is therefore loaded with intrigue and deceit.

Jacob tells his blind father that he is Esau the firstborn and that he is ready to be blessed. There comes a tender moment at this point that is worth pointing out:

> Then his father Isaac said to him, 'Come here, my son, and kiss me.' So he went to him and kissed him. When Isaac caught the smell of his clothes, he blessed him and said, 'Ah, the smell of my son is like the smell of a field that the Lord has blessed.'
>
> (Genesis 27.26–27)

John Trent and Gary Smalley tell us that this passage demonstrates some of the common elements in conveying blessings and in particular father and mother blessings. Pronouncing blessings should include a meaningful and appropriate touch. Normally this would be the laying on of hands but in Isaac's case he gives the invitation to come close and kiss. The blessing is to be spoken aloud. In addition there should be a high value conveyed to the one being blessed. Isaac complimented his son by saying that he smelled like a field that God had blessed. Blessings should include a specific and special future. Isaac tells his son that God will give him the riches of the ground, an abundance of grain and wine and that he would have the obedience of nations (Gen. 27.26–29).[4]

We can only wonder what impact all this had on Jacob as he knelt there deceiving his father. We looked into his life in the previous chapter, but let us remind ourselves that the effect of this blessing pronouncement did not fully come into operation until he confessed his name and nature in his desperation to be blessed by God himself. He got honest with himself in the end and so entered into the blessings intended for him.

Now comes the pain of the son who was not blessed. Esau discovers his brother's treachery, tells Isaac all about it and clamours to be blessed by his father also. 'My father! Can't you also bless me?' He even asks if his father has only one blessing to give his sons (Gen. 27.33–34). The account describes this as a loud and bitter cry. Isaac does bless Esau but not with what he wanted. He describes how he will serve his brother but that the day will come when he will be free of Jacob's yoke. In a way this is a mangle of a blessing story. No one went home happy and even Jacob has to flee for his life and so leaves the family home for 20 years. It is the context that is all wrong. It demonstrates that for blessings to be received well there must be an honesty and integrity between the one who gives and the one who receives the blessing. I think it quite likely Isaac would have given the same blessings to both sons even had he known the true identity of the one he was blessing. Indeed a recurring theme in these father-blessing stories is that it is not the eldest son who gets the blessing he might have been expecting. Isaac says emphatically that he had blessed Jacob and that he would stay blessed (Gen. 27.33).

Jacob

Jacob is distinguished in Scripture as blessing not only his 12 sons but also his two grandsons, the children of Joseph. As with Isaac, this all takes place towards the end of his life, and the context is passing on to his sons and grandsons what God had given him down the years. First comes the blessings for Joseph's sons, Ephraim and Manasseh. Once again the scene is intimate, with touching and kissing, laying on of hands and speaking of words. Once again there is the recurring theme of the younger being served by the elder (Gen. 48.15–20). The final blessing becomes, 'In your name will Israel pronounce this blessing: "May God make you like Ephraim and Manasseh."' As we shall see, these words have since become the standard blessing for fathers to pray over their sons at the Shabbat meal.

Jacob's final blessings spoken over his 12 sons who gathered about his deathbed are a mixed blessing to say the least (Gen. 49.1–28). They come more in the context of prophetic pronouncements of their future destinies. He basically says that Reuben his firstborn is a disappointment, a man who has lost his honour through immoral conduct. Simeon and Levi are no better. Issachar is described as a scrawny donkey, Dan as a snake by the roadside and Benjamin as a ravenous wolf. Such words would hardly endear any father to his son. Only Judah and Joseph are praised for their trust in God.

The helpful clue behind all this is in the closing summary of these blessings: 'All these are the twelve tribes of Israel, and this is what their father said to them when he blessed them, *giving each the blessing appropriate to him*' (v. 28, my italics). Blessing others is not wishful thinking or a spurious platitude, but a God-inspired pronouncement for well-being. Perhaps there was hope in Jacob's heart that his pronouncements would serve as a wake-up call to his sons. This is why I think it perfectly acceptable to bless our lost sons and daughters with words such as:

> I bless you with knowing just how much you are loved by me and by the God who made you. I bless you with experiencing the heart of God in your life that you may grow into all the fullness of life that he has for you.

We are to think about what we pronounce over our children and take note of their lives as we do so. Our blessings can take the form of longings and exhortations as well as the asking for increase of favour on those who already walk in God's ways. This brings us to the father's blessing over his only begotten son Jesus.

The blessing over Jesus

> And a voice came from heaven: 'You are my Son, whom I love; with you I am well pleased.' (Luke 3.22)

I remember speaking on this theme of blessing and affirmation to a group of clergy from some of the Oxford colleges. I asked them to imagine how Jesus might have felt to have these words spoken over him by his father. There was a pronounced silence until one of them said something like, 'He must have known what it was to fulfil that for which he was predestined. Namely that he was the once for all sacrifice for the sins of the whole world.' While I could not argue with his theology, it wasn't really answering the question. One of the female deacons present suddenly said, 'He must have felt bloody marvellous! I wouldn't mind my dad saying such wonderful things to me!' I thought she had it right. In terms of the Protestant work ethic, Jesus had done nothing to deserve the words of blessing. He had not healed anyone up to this moment; not spoken powerful and comforting words to anyone; not converted gallons of water into excellent Merlot! He was just being the son of his father and that alone was worthy of affirmation. Once again we ask ourselves, 'How many of us would have loved hearing such good blessing words from our parents?' I am sure they empowered and encouraged Jesus to face the onslaughts and battles that were to come immediately after this momentous time, as he tramped the desert and lived with the growing hostilities and plots that surrounded him. The blessing of the Father sustained his life and helped keep him on track.

Jack Hayford writes that the blessing of children has a determinative effect on the child's life:

> The principle is clear, God has given parents the privilege and power to speak blessing upon their children and with that blessing to advance life and health and growth, joy and self-confidence. We need to learn to steward this privilege as a dynamic aspect of raising our children and blessing them in any way we possibly can.[5]

If spoken blessings so fortified Jesus, how much more are we in need of such intentional blessings on our own lives? As we noted earlier from the comment by Aaron Fruh, we live in a world with so many unblessed children. No matter how old they are, if they are our children we can make up for lost time and bless them when we have the opportunity. We will see later in this chapter that we can also pronounce these blessings over our children and grandchildren even if they are far away from us. Blessings can travel across continents and seas!

We have been looking at the rhythm of the father's blessing in Scripture. Now we turn to how the blessing of Jacob over Joseph's sons has become a model for the blessing of children in Jewish households.

Sabbath blessings of children

If you enter any home of any Orthodox Jewish family anywhere in the world during a Friday evening Shabbat celebration, you will see the parents regularly blessing their children. It is the father who begins this once the meal is over. He calls his sons to his side, lays his hands on their heads and proclaims the blessing, 'May you be like Ephraim and Manasseh'. As in many Old Testament names, they have a particular meaning. Manasseh means 'making forgetful', which is coupled to the explanation spoken by Joseph, 'For God has made me forget all my trouble and all my father's household' (Gen. 41.51). Ephraim means 'fruitfulness', and again Joseph explains why: 'It is because God has made me fruitful in the land of my suffering' (Gen. 41.52). Joseph named his sons as a faith reflection on all his painful story, with its misery and amazing triumphs. We already know that this blessing was first spoken by the elderly Jacob over his grandsons. By it was meant that all Israel in the future will bless their own children with this blessing: 'God cause you to forget the pain of your past and make you fruitful and prosperous in the future.' And so Orthodox Jewish fathers bless their sons with this same intention of wholeness and health for their futures. I think it is a blessing all fathers could and should pray over our children.

The mothers in such households will, in turn, gather their daughters around them and lay their hands on their heads and proclaim the blessing from Ruth: 'The LORD make the woman who is coming to your house like Rachel and Leah, the two who built the house of Israel; and may you prosper in Ephrathah and be famous in Bethlehem' (4.11 NKJV). This is a reference to the fact that between them the sisters Rachel and Leah gave birth to eight sons of the patriarch Jacob. They were consequently honoured as the mothers of Israel. The blessing of daughters in Orthodox Jewish homes today is not so much that they might have many sons but that they should be endowed with all the good qualities of their parents and forebears.

At the heart of such family blessings is the necessary and healing touch of celebration and honouring. I learnt long ago that what we do not celebrate shrinks with lack of affirmation. It is not just true for individuals but churches, tribes and nations also. In blessing our children we honour them and give value and dignity to their lives. If we give such blessings then I believe God honours our intentions and uses them to encourage our children to step up and into the honoured and celebrated life. Celebration is not flattery but the recognition of our children's worth as being truly human, and the focus of the incredible love of God their father.

Aaron Fruh goes so far as to encourage all parents to devise and hold regular blessing rituals for their household. His starting point is the reference in 2 Samuel of David returning home to bless his household (6.20). He says it must have been pretty much as is still the case in Orthodox Jewish homes.[6] He suggests six practical ingredients for these events, ranging from blessing the love between the parents, focusing blessings on all material possessions such as cars, house, computers and the garden, blessing the work of the family, to blessing unborn children and future husbands and wives of the children. If this feels somewhat old-fashioned and rather twee, it might be more to do with how much we have lost the family dynamic in modern society than with something out of date and no longer needed. It is a fact of postmodern life that we stretch our hearts between the polarities of increasing fragmentation and the increased desire to belong to something. According to the researcher George Barna, the matter is compounded within church families as the trend over the years has been to abdicate responsibility for the moral and spiritual growth of children to the church and out of the home. This is true despite the statistic that 85 per cent of Christian parents state that it is their calling to raise their children to be responsible citizens of the faith and of society.[7] Naturally no one is disputing the role of the Church to raise up mature individuals of the Christian faith, but Barna does have a point.

I think we would do our children a great service if we rediscovered the ministry of fathers and mothers blessing them. I have discovered that it is never too late for parents to begin blessing their children, even after they have left the family home. I would go so far as to say that it has transformed the way I pray for my children, especially when they are also far away from practising the Christian faith in which they were raised.

Blessing the children to come home to Jesus

It is a familiar story that there are many Christian parents with children who did not or do not share their walk with Jesus. Some have just fallen out with the Church and their spiritual lives are on hold or in slow decline. Others have rebelled and turned their backs on the faith in which they were raised. No doubt there are many reasons for this and often it is a consequence of the fathers and mothers getting it all wrong. What follows is sometimes an uneasy peace as people try and get on with their lives and stay connected with their parents because they still love them and the parents also love their children.

I wonder if you are such a parent; if you have made the same mistake I have when you pray for your children? My prayers were very adversarial. I prayed in a sort of fix-bayonets methodology whereby I came against the dark things in my children's lives, asked the Lord to bind such things and set them free, show them the error of their ways and challenge them to come back to Jesus. The only problem is that the so-called unsaved are not stupid! I am sure they know how we pray for them and they respond by entrenching themselves against the tirade of our battle prayers. My 'mighty praying' seemed only to push them further away from me and any interest in discussing their faith journey.

The turning point came some years ago when my daughter, Emma, was expecting her first child. I visited her in her home near Norwich on the day before she gave birth to beautiful Rosie, my first grandchild. As I was nearing the end of my visit and getting ready to go on retreat with some very dear friends, I asked Emma if I could lay hands on her and pray for her unborn child. She said, 'No'! I was very upset and I am sure she could sense it. 'You don't mind if I say "No", do you?' she asked. I told her that I did mind but that she was a mature woman and I respected her decision. So I left and went to take part in the retreat.

When it came to my turn I shared this episode and how terribly hurt I felt, how useless a father I must be that my daughter would not let me pray with her, how I felt my world crashing in on me. If I could not help my own daughter to come to the faith she was raised in, what gave me the right to try to help someone else's daughter to come to that same faith? Then my friend Mike, possibly my best friend after my wife Roz, said, 'I know Emma, your daughter. Why don't we all bless her. Let's imagine she is just across the road from us and we are shouting out the blessings of God on her.' So six men stood around me and shouted out at the top of their voices:

> Emma! You are beautiful and wonderfully made and God so loves you. We bless you with knowing how much you are loved by God. We bless you as a mother with great patience and joy. We bless you with your father's love. Emma! You are a wonderful girl and we bless you with wonder and love in Jesus' name.

I sheepishly thanked them for their care and prayers but had zero expectation that anything would come of them. At this point we took a break and put the kettle on for a cup of tea, and it was then that my mobile phone rang. It was my daughter Emma calling me from the hospital. She joyfully told me that she was sitting in the ward holding my granddaughter in her lap. I broke down in almost uncontrollable crying and tried to tell her how special she was and what a great mother she would be. She interrupted me at some stage by saying that she was sorry she had not let me pray for her and bless her daughter. It sounds a bit pompous now but she said that when I lay hands on people things usually happen and she had enough problems in her life without my creating more! I told her I understood and that Roz and I would come over and see her and Rosie as soon as we could. My daughter is a wonderful woman and a really marvellous mother, and it was only after this moment of blessing prayer that slowly we began to draw closer together than ever before. We still have miles to travel but things are so much better now, for which I truly thank God. I have since made it a regular feature of my prayers to bless my children, family and friends – rather than pray my former battle prayers. I have also made a point of sharing this insight in my ministry wherever I go. There have always been faithful Christian parents who share their tears with me and tell how they and their children have drifted far apart and had little or no contact for years. Then they have taken up the blessing prayers for their children and call out to them – as if they were just across the road and they want to catch their attention. God has been very faithful and responded to these prayers, as a result of which many children have come home to their parents and subsequently to a renewed faith in Jesus.

I have many such stories I could share but here are just two. The first is of a woman in a Pentecostal church near Manchester who asked if she could pray for her son-in-law in this way. According to her he was obnoxious and very unlikeable, and she could never understand what her daughter saw in him. They had all argued and fallen out years ago and she now only saw her grandchildren on rare occasions. I can see her now in the body of the congregation, calling out her blessings on this son-in-law as everyone else was busy blessing their own families. As she was blessing, her mobile phone went off and she immediately stopped praying to answer it. Then I heard her cry out so loudly, 'I don't believe it! I'm in church right now calling out your name asking God to bless you.' She came and told me that he had decided to ring her on impulse at that moment to mend fences with her because his wife was so depressed by the situation between them.

The second story happened at a healing conference with Judith MacNutt in Vail, Colorado where I was preaching on blessing. At the end of the conference people were invited to share any healing they had received from God. One grandfather came to the front and said that last night he had been reconciled with a son he had not spoken to for over 20 years. He had gone out into the night, called out his son's name, blessed him with his father's love and asked him to forgive him for his pride. His mobile phone then began to ring, and it was his son. Apparently his son had been drawn to enter a church as he walked by that night. He heard them singing old hymns he remembered from his childhood when he had gone to church with his parents. As he entered the church the man welcoming visitors had asked him if he knew how much his father loved him. The welcomer was thinking of God but the son was thinking of his dad with whom he had argued so long ago. It prompted him there and then to phone his sister to get his father's number and ring him.

Now I cannot claim that all blessing prayers have a mobile-phone conclusion to them, nor that they are answered as swiftly. Yet children seem to know if their parents bless them, and deep within their hearts is the recognition that they not only need such blessings but want them too. This was affirmed for me when I took part in another conference with Judith MacNutt, this time in Denver. Judith approached me and said they were now going to offer the father and mother blessings to anyone who wanted it.[8] However, before the people came forward to receive these blessings, I was invited to read out the father's apology and blessing preparation. When I had completed this about a dozen men of various ages, the youngest 18, stood in a row at the front of the hall and waited for people to come. I confess I thought it wouldn't work and that some of the men at the front were going to be embarrassed and stand there waiting without receiving any customers. How wrong I was! Over half the people, men and women, came forward to receive the father's blessing. I watched in humbled appreciation as the 18-year-old man embraced a very old man and gave him a father's blessing. Then I went forward and received a warm hug and a simple blessing of 'Be blessed with my father's heart of love for you, my son'. I was suddenly transported through the whole of my childhood and beyond with a sharpened awareness that I had never been blessed or celebrated by my father at any time in my life. It was not because he was a bad person but because he too was a wounded child who had never received a father's blessing. I stood there weeping for my father and then silently blessing him wherever he was in eternity.

Choosing the words of blessing for our children

Only yesterday I listened to someone reciting that amazing poem by William Butler Yeats, 'When You Are Old'. I was struck by some of the words in the second verse:

> But one man loved the pilgrim soul in you
> and loved the sorrows of your changing face.

I realize Yeats is writing of the love that spans the years of ageing between two who love each other so well, but I suddenly thought that it is equally true of a father and mother and especially of the father heart of God for his children. Our children will have mixed fortunes in life – there will be times of flourishing, times of wounding and disappointments. Yet through all times our father and mother hearts can and do reach out to bless them, come what may. So what words should we use to bless our children without it sounding like flattery or wishful thinking?

I cannot put words into your mouths but I often ask parents, 'What is the most important thing you want God to do for your son or daughter? What is it they need to flourish as the person you know them to be or that they can be?' Whatever your answer to these two questions, turn them into blessing prayers and be as bold and directive as you dare! Let us imagine your son lacks confidence; then your pronouncement would be, 'Jim, I bless you with confidence in your life that you will flourish as God intended you to.' Let us imagine your son or daughter is that gifted prodigal who is far away from home and God. Your pronouncement would be, 'Carol, I bless you with knowing how much you are loved and I bless you with the heart to come home to Jesus and I bless you with my father's [or mother's] heart of love for you.'

It is always a good thing to think and pray about what is suitable to put into your blessing pronouncement so that when you speak it out it will be with as much faith and expectation as you are able. Jack Hayford suggests a number of principal ingredients in all blessing prayers for our children:

- Our words must affirm and approve.
- We must commend and compliment.
- We must speak out of love and affection.
- Our blessings should invoke hope for our children and confidence in them of our love and acceptance of them.
- We should focus on support and faith rather than pain and disappointments.[9]

These are very useful guidelines to help us construct our blessing prayers for our children. Let me underline that these blessings are best said with and over our children, but for many of us this is not possible as they are far from home. I encourage you to say them in faith out loud, even if you are separated by whole continents from your children! I have been greatly encouraged by the many who have shared with me the answers to blessing prayers that have come back to them. If it helps, imagine your son or daughter is on the other side of the street and you are calling out your prayers to catch their attention. Make this the action of your faith and call out your blessings on your children now.

Conclusion

We may not know what to say in the blessing of our children, and if that is the case I strongly encourage you to take the Aaronic blessing that we have already discussed and make it the personal blessing prayer for your children. Make sure you name them, and wherever they are, with you or far away from you, speak out this blessing for them.

> Peter/Jane, the Lord bless you and keep you;
> Peter/Jane, the Lord make his face shine on
> you and be gracious to you;
> Peter/Jane, the Lord turn his face toward you and
> give you peace.

8

Blessings in battle

A blessing is regarded as positively altering reality.[1]

One of the most colourful if not bizarre episodes in the Bible is that of King Balak of Moab endeavouring to halt the conquering Israelites in their tracks by cursing them (Num. 22—24). The irony is that the Israelites originally had no intention of invading Moab because they had been given divine instructions not to (Deut. 2.9). Balak therefore summons Balaam, son of Beor, to open the assault on the approaching invaders. Roy Gane describes Balaam as someone with an international reputation for pronouncing effective blessings, and when it comes to curses, you could say he is a world-class maledictorian.[2] Balak says of him, 'I know that whoever you bless is blessed, and whoever you curse is cursed' (Num. 22.6b).

The battle lines are drawn and the winner, it seems, is going to be the one who can pronounce the effective curses. We are not told how but it is apparent Balak does not expect the curse to destroy Israel, only soften up or disturb them to give his fighting troops a chance for victory.

This is not the place to expound the story in full and we shall focus just on the main elements.[3] Balaam finds he can do no other than bless the Israelites, even though he has been commissioned to curse and is offered all manner of wealth to do so. He insists he can only say what the Lord gives him to say, which is to bless (Num. 22.12, 18, 35, 38; 23.3, 8, 12, 20; 24.13). He goes on to bless the Israelites four times! Needless to say Balak is exasperated at this outcome. The other important element in this story is that in being blessed, the Israelites cannot be effectively cursed. This point is repeated in the Old Testament in connection with Abraham and his descendants.

> I will make you into a great nation, and I will bless you;
> I will make your name great, and you will be a blessing.
> I will bless those who bless you, and whoever curses you
> I will curse;
> And all peoples on earth will be blessed through you.
> (Genesis 12.2–3)

Naturally this divine protection and benefit was conditional on keeping the covenant committed to them. John H. Walton writes that individuals may choose to step outside God's covenant-keeping promises but this did not alter the fact that God was going to fulfil his divine purposes through his corporate chosen people, which was to reveal his blessing in the world no matter what happened.[4]

The blessing protection

The Lord's firm resolve to bless and protect the children of Abraham also extends to Christians who, through faith in Christ, are the children of Abraham (Gal. 3.29). We could therefore take to heart the fourth blessing of Balaam that says, 'The Lord their God is with them; the shout of the King is among them' (Num. 23.21b). Gane says of this: 'With the divine king in our camp we have ultimate "social security".'[5]

I think we need to take more seriously than we do that as Christians we have the protection of being the blessed people of God. We are not sitting ducks who are easily toppled by the curses others pronounce over us. As the writer of Proverbs states, 'an undeserved curse does not come to rest' (Prov. 26.2b). If we are walking in obedience to God the principle of blessing protects us from the power of spiritual assault through curses. I remember being in one particular worship service when the words, 'You are more secure than you think you are', were impressed on my mind. After some quiet reflection and prayer I thought it right to share these words with the congregation. The pastor of the church responded with relief and enthusiasm. He shared with me that the church had being praying fervently about its own difficulties in engaging in effective evangelism in the neighbourhood. During this time of prolonged prayer someone had said that the reason for the lack of results was because the church was situated very close to a local Masonic Hall. This person was of the opinion that the church was cursed through its proximity to that building. Consequently the church had become overfocused on praying against such alleged spiritual powers. However, the pastor had never been comfortable with this explanation as he thought it undermined the power of God to protect his own. As a result of all this we decided to get proactive about being the blessed community and decided to pronounce blessing prayers over the church. I cannot now remember exactly what we prayed that day but it would have been something like the following:

> We bless this church with the blessings of God so that it becomes the church the Lord has called it to be.
> We bless this church with an increase in knowing the presence of God.
> We bless this church with release and renewal in the Holy Spirit.
> We bless this church with a new-found love and liberty in Jesus Christ.
> We bless this church with God's protection.
> We bless this church with a new power to share the good news in this community.
> We bless this church in the name of the Father, the Son and the Holy Spirit.

In due time the church was able to let go of its sense of oppression and failure as new insights and ways of reaching out were engaged and it began to grow.

Whatever your opinion on the rights and wrongs of Freemasonry for Christians, and while not undermining the reality of spiritual battle, we must not surrender the fact that the people of faith are kept by the power of God. Neither must we disregard that as blessed people it is no guarantee that we do not suffer persecution (cf. for example Matt. 5.11 and Luke 21.12). Nor does it imply that the wicked will never be more prosperous than the faithful. However, it is the bedrock of our Christian faith that the Lord ultimately decrees our final destinies. The final chapter of all our stories is that God will get back his family fully restored and living on the renewed earth he has prepared for us.

Not only are blessings our ground of protection but they are also our weapons in adversity that we use to keep ourselves connected with the witness of Jesus in a fallen world.

The blessing weapon of witness

One of the most important books in the Bible on Christian suffering and perseverance is that of the First Epistle of Peter. He was writing to the scattered Christian communities, many of whom were beginning to draw the fires of hostility from both religious and political quarters. Peter was concerned not only that they kept their faith intact but also that in doing so they would be witnesses to the Jesus quality of living for others. He wrote, 'Do not repay evil with evil or insult with insult. On the contrary, repay evil with blessing, because to this you were called so that you may inherit a blessing' (1 Pet. 3.9; cf. Rom. 12.14). You can imagine Peter remembering the words of Jesus in the so-called Sermon on the Plain, 'I say: Love your enemies, do good to those who hate you, bless those who curse you, pray for those who mistreat you' (Luke 6.27–28). Jesus encourages us into a threefold response when we are suffering at the hands of others, to do good, to bless and to pray. He lived this quality of life himself. There would also have been the example of his last words of forgiveness for his enemies when he suffered on the cross (Luke 23.34) and the dying words of the first martyr Stephen that were so similar to those of the Saviour he loved (Acts 7.60).

Darrell L. Bock describes this as a calling to exceptional love and mercy.[6] Such a generosity to our enemies is not the usual response people are expected to make. It requires a supernatural grace. Yet this is our high calling as Christians and disciples of Jesus. However, when Christians respond in this way it is a powerful witness to the love of Christ that carries with it the invitation to others to be changed into his likeness also. Who can forget the impact of Gordon Wilson's supreme act of forgiveness towards the unknown bombers within the IRA who slaughtered his daughter and many others on Remembrance Sunday in Enniskillen in Northern Ireland? As he lay in the rubble following the explosion he held the hand of his daughter Anne Marie until she died. It was in that moment he chose not to spend the rest of his life holding bitterness against his enemies but chose to forgive them. What followed was amazing. Wilson received over a quarter of a million letters in the weeks that followed, the vast bulk thanking him for his example and many sharing their writers' own difficulties with forgiving others. His actions had prompted them to think again. He also received death threats from people who had also suffered similar losses and thought Wilson was letting the IRA off from being accountable for their atrocities. Other threats were because his actions had exposed the evil that was perpetrated on the public for what it was and not some justifiable political necessity. The Queen mentioned Gordon Wilson in her Christmas speech that year and hoped we could all learn to love our neighbour as he undoubtedly had.

The blessing of those who persecute us touches on a number of issues: the need to witness to those in peril from their own actions; to see our enemies as those whom we are called especially to love; and to stay connected to our own calling to be the holy and blessed people of God.

Witness to those in peril from their own actions

Let us be frank: it is not a pleasant experience to be attacked by others. It is very hard to resist the temptation to give as good as we get. Paul, in writing to the Romans, goes so far as to say that should there be no awakening to grace to our doing good to our enemies, the ultimate outcome for them is destruction (Rom. 12.20). There is nothing neutral in being a blessing to those who persecute us. However, this is not our desired goal and it should trouble us deeply that our offers of grace do not bring our enemies to repentance and transformation. Rather our blessings are designed by God to challenge others to wake up to the goodness of Jesus seen, it is to be hoped, in our actions and responses.

A personal example of this is the story of my growing relationship over the years with my brother-in-law Bobby. He worked for Cammell Laird Shipyards in Birkenhead and in his spare time played drums for a jazz band called The Blue Magnolias. Bobby was a man with a great sense of humour but it could so easily turn into ridicule. He took great delight in focusing his ability and disapproval on my Christian faith. I did not really help matters either because I think I was pushy in sharing my faith and took great exception when he would make fun of my beliefs. I didn't like him very much and I think it was mutual. When I came to pray for Bobby I treated him as an enemy fortress that needed to be stormed by the power of God. Needless to say there were no outward signs that my prayers were having any good effect. As time passed I got rather angry and depressed at my lack of results and my prayers became even more aggressive.

However, there came a time when I felt God stopping me in my tracks from praying. I was challenged to pray another way. The thought came strongly to my mind, 'Can you imagine Bobby living as a Christian? Bless that to him.' I refocused my prayers and began to bless Bobby's life. I blessed him so that his skill with words would become something to help rather than put down. I did my best to change my heart attitude towards him also and with God's help things began to change. Then came a moment of high drama.

Bobby developed a rather dangerous tumour of the brain and ended up in the intensive care unit of Walton Hospital in Liverpool. He was in a drug-controlled coma for most of the time but at others he was heavily sedated. It was during one of these periods that he began to call out my name repeatedly. My sister phoned me and asked me to come and pray with him. When I arrived at the hospital and approached his bedside he looked much smaller than usual. I lightly laid hands on him and prayed, 'Wherever you are Bobby, I know that Jesus is in there with you and I bless his healing presence to your life.' Nothing happened immediately but very shortly afterwards his condition dramatically improved and he soon came home with all the tumour removed from his brain. The biggest miracle for me was the noticeable change in his attitude towards me and towards God. Gone was the ridicule and sarcasm and in its place was this lovely, warm and generous man whom I came to love and respect so much. We are the best of all pals – he is supportive of me and has grown a gentle generosity that endears him to everyone. There are more miles to go in his walk with God but he is definitely on the pathway.

We need to learn that when we bless those who are giving us a bad time it is a window of opportunity in their lives to see the love God has for them and to reach for it. I now encourage people when they have similar difficult relationships to ask God to show them that person changed by the touch of Jesus and to pray and bless for what they see. I am almost tempted to say that if we cannot imagine it, how can we truly pray for it or bless it? So it seems the first transformation in blessing others is in ourselves. Such blessing prayers are no guarantee that our opponents will change but it is the desired purpose of God that our blessings will bring them to this. Mind you, the challenge is also on us. It is not enough to pronounce blessings, we must also live them by doing good in any way we can to those we bless.

See our enemies as those we are specially to love

It was Michael Marshall, the former Bishop of Woolwich and Rector of Holy Trinity Church in Sloane Street, London, who once told me that the good news is the love of God going out of his way to find us and bring us home. Paul echoes this truth in his letter to the Romans when he describes our experience of saving grace as like enemies being reconciled to God by the death of his son Jesus (Rom. 5.11). We may see enemies but God sees lost sons and daughters worth rescuing. In being blessed by the love of God we find our way back home to the heart of God. Similarly, I think God calls us to bless our enemies as our need to engage in love's great challenge and calling. The action of blessing those who oppose us is equally for our benefit, that we may not be consumed by the scars of battle but transformed by the love of God that we share with them.

Stay connected to a holy and blessed lifestyle

On a practical level I find it very hard to dislike someone I am blessing. It is impossible to bless properly if we harbour resentment and anger towards the other. When Peter exhorts us to be the people that bless, he links it with a quote from Psalm 34.

> Whoever wants to embrace life
> and see the day fill up with good, Here's what you do:
> Say nothing evil or hurtful; Snub evil and cultivate good;
> run after peace for all you're worth.
> God looks on all this with approval,
> listening and responding well to what he's asked.
> (1 Peter 3.10–12 *The Message*)

Not only is blessing a wake-up call for the one with whom we struggle but also for us, and a reminder that we have a calling to be holy people. It is so easy in times of spiritual battle to become too enmeshed in how bad things are and soured or corroded by the struggles we face. There have been too many casualties where Christians facing persecution and hostilities have become hardened by the effects of battle. Their hope and joy in the Lord has been seriously undermined and they have become tired and disillusioned. Quite a few church leaders have given up their ministries because of the collateral damage incurred in wrestling with those who have opposed them. While we do need to take seriously the place of rest and retreat and renewal from the wear and tear of serving in a fallen world, we must also take seriously the resource of blessing when in battle. It is in blessing that we are rescued from despondency and being overshadowed by the power and pains of the conflict itself.

We also need to get the balance right between the times when we should bless and when we should engage in battle prayers against our true enemies. Paul also reminds us that the wrestling side of spiritual battle is not principally against people but spiritual powers:

> For our struggle is not against flesh and blood, but against the rulers, against the authorities, against the powers of this dark world and against the spiritual forces of evil in the heavenly realms. (Ephesians 6.12)

There is a necessary place for prayers of holy aggression against the spiritual powers and it is perfectly acceptable to pray to break and bind their hold over humanity, however we imagine this. Yet we must not be displaced into thinking that we come against human beings in quite the same way. Our call to be the people that bless is a weapon both for protection of ourselves and also for the redeeming of our enemies. It is a protection for ourselves because not only does it protect us from the power of curses and other spiritual contamination but also anchors us in the heart of God. It is not only in blessing our enemies that we stay on track, it is also in learning to bless God.

Blessing God

Without a doubt Scripture is replete with examples of people blessing God for his goodness and greatness. The book of Psalms is a rich source of these blessings and the overall context certainly seems to be that of worship and celebration of God. The following are just a few examples, but it would serve us well to explore many more in the Bible and weave them into the pattern of our worship moments.

> Enter into His gates with thanksgiving,
> And into His courts with praise,
> Be thankful to Him, and bless His name. (Psalm 100.4 NKJV)

Bless the LORD, O my soul;
And all that is within me, bless His holy name!
Bless the LORD, O my soul,
And forget not all His benefits. (Psalm 103.1–2 NKJV)

I lift you high in praise, my God, O my King!
and I'll bless your name into eternity.
I'll bless you every day,
and keep it up from now to eternity.
(Psalm 145.1–2 *The Message*)

As there is so much in the Bible about blessing God we do well to ask ourselves what is the purpose and therapeutic effect of such blessings. John Piper writes that when God blesses us we are thereby helped and strengthened and made better off than we were before, but when we bless God he is not helped or strengthened or made better off.[7] God is after all perfect and complete and indeed the chief and inexhaustible blesser!

Therefore it is quite clear that when we bless God we are recognizing God's great richness, strength and favour to us and also expressing our thanks and praise and delight in seeing and experiencing the very truths we extol. We are told in Psalm 22.3 that God inhabits or is enthroned on the praises of his people. It is so interesting that this verse comes straight after a cry of despair that Jesus himself used when suffering on the cross: 'My God, my God, why have you forsaken me?' (Matt. 27.46). When we come to the end of Psalm 22, however, the writer is back on track, refocused on the God whose purposes will still be fulfilled in his life (vv. 25–31). Could it be that the choice to bless and praise God helped the psalmist to stay connected to the God who was with him in his darkness? It certainly seems that this was Jesus' purpose when he took the opening verse of Psalm 22 and used those words to vocalize his agony of grief and suffering.

Another example of being kept from losing focus on God in times of suffering and battle can be found in Psalm 34. David wrote, 'I will bless the LORD at all times; His praise shall continually be in my mouth' (Ps. 34.1 NKJV). The prefix to the psalm states that it is a psalm of David when he pretended madness before Abimelech, who drove him away and he departed. This psalm was sung at a time in David's life when he was friendless, among a hostile power about to invade his country and about to be sent into exile. What kept him true to the purposes of God in his life was to choose to bless and praise God, which undoubtedly raised his spirits and kept him from sinking into despair.

Blessing God enables us to stay better connected with the very truths we are extolling. It is not a self-help technique we can simply turn on but a way of life commended to us from saints who have gone before.[8] I have always been challenged and encouraged by the fact that when Paul and Silas were in the Philippian prison after receiving a savage beating, they found space to pray and praise and sing hymns at midnight (Acts 16.22–25)!

- To bless God is to walk in the Spirit.
- To bless God is to reach out for more of his presence in our lives.
- To bless God is to be open to more of his anointing on our faith endeavours.
- To bless God is to stay on track and in tune with his calling on our lives.
- To bless God is to resist giving in to the darkness that surrounds us in battle.
- To bless God is to worship him and be thankful for all he is and has done for us.

I bless the name of Jesus, he is the King and Saviour of my life.
I bless the Lord with all my heart for he alone is mighty to save.
I bless the God of my salvation, his praises will garrison my spirit.
I bless my heavenly Father because he has brought me home to myself.
I bless the Lord because he stays by my side and is the light in my darkness.
I bless Father, Son and Holy Spirit. Amen.

9

Blessing the land

Almighty God,
whose will it is that the earth and the sea
 should bear fruit in due season:
bless the labours of those who work on land and sea,
grant us a good harvest
and the grace always to rejoice in your fatherly care;
through Jesus Christ your Son our Lord,
who is alive and reigns with you,
in the unity of the Holy Spirit,
one God, now and for ever. Amen. (*Common Worship*)[1]

According to Scripture the first recipients of the blessing of God were the birds in the air and the fish in the sea (Gen. 1.22). After creating them on the fifth day, and seeing how good it was for them to be alive, God blessed what he made so that they would be fruitful and increase in number.

On the sixth day of creation when humankind was created they received a similar blessing and commission to be fruitful and increase in number (Gen. 1.28–30). It is interesting to note that the blessing conferred on humanity links directly with the blessing conferred on the birds of the air and the fish of the sea. We are blessed to steward the earth's resources not just for our own needs but that the blessing on creation may be honoured. It is on this critical balance of respective blessings that hinges our rightful stewardship of the land and its resources. In *Blackfoot Physics*, the holistic physicist F. David Peat recounts his time spent among the Native American tribes of Turtle Island in Canada. He gives a fascinating account of how the culture of that indigenous people was to give thanks to the deity for providing food and game after a successful hunt. They also thanked the fish and animals for their gift of life and sustenance that their death had given them.[2] This may appear primitive to our modern sensibilities but it illustrates the principle of respective blessings and exerts a powerful restraint on overindulgence in reducing the stocks of fish and game on the land.

It is this link of the blessings that is continued throughout Scripture. At the climax of the New Testament we are treated to the spectacular vision of the renewed heaven and earth linked to restored community called the new Jerusalem (Rev. 21.1–3). Paul speaks of creation groaning and longing for such a day to come and that it would not come until God's healing purposes had been fulfilled in humanity (Rom. 8.19–21). The consummation of God's master plan is for the full reinstatement of the twin blessings of flourishing and fulfilment on humanity and the creation.

One of the bridges between initial creation and final consummation is the subject of land as gift and sacrament. As we have already noted, the blessing bestowed on Abraham was the link between serving the purposes of God and flourishing as a people in the land of promise. However, it was essential that land was understood as a gift from God and not the prize for services rendered. Yet as Walter Brueggemann reminds us, 'gifted land is also covenanted land'.[3] There was a holy pattern of living required to abide securely and fruitfully in this land. This is made abundantly clear throughout the story that unfolds in the Old Testament. The book of Joshua recounts the battles to take and maintain the land, and once in the land the book closes with the reminder, 'Not one of the LORD's good promises to the house of Israel failed; every one was fulfilled' (Josh. 21.45). The Deuteronomist in compiling the law codes by which this community would live in the land stated:

> When the LORD your God brings you into the land he swore to your fathers, to Abraham, Isaac and Jacob, to give you – a land with large, flourishing cities you did not build, houses filled with all kinds of good things you did not provide, wells you did not dig, and vineyards and olive groves you did not plant – then when you eat and are satisfied, *be careful that you do not forget the Lord*, who brought you out of Egypt, out of the land of slavery. (Deuteronomy 6.10–12, my italics)

Alongside the laws were also the marking-post ceremonies of celebration in the land. These were the feasts of Passover, Firstfruits, Weeks,

Trumpets and Tabernacles (Lev. 23.4–44). The marker posts were those reminders of the connection of fruitful land and the saving relationship with Yahweh who made it all possible through his gift of land and presence. 'To forget God was to risk harming the land and facing the possibility of eviction.'[4] Compare the stark exhortation in Deuteronomy 28 of blessings and curses according to how the people kept faith with God and the land:

> You will be blessed in the city and blessed in the country . . . The LORD will grant you abundant prosperity – in the fruit of your womb, the young of your livestock and the crops of your ground – in the land he swore to your ancestors to give you. (vv. 3, 11)

> You will be cursed in the city and cursed in the country . . . The fruit of your womb will be cursed, and the crops of your land. (vv. 16, 18)

All these Scriptures bring together the twin blessings we have referred to and living in obedience to God's covenant principles and laws.

> The land was not a passive bystander to the affairs of the covenant community but a player in the game. At the heart of this link is Yahweh who challenges us to live according to his principles on the land which is his gift to us. It is not simply that what we do on the land affects the land for good or ill; it is how we relate to the presence of God which affects the land, because land is the living link with the presence of God.[5]

The most devastating and yet transforming example of this was the exile and the loss of the gift of land. It is stamped on the Bible as a permanent reminder of what happened when the covenant community lost its reason to live in the land when they abandoned their founding principles. Yet even in exile they are challenged to return to the covenant and find flourishing in a foreign land because Yahweh is Lord of all land. It is these principles of holy living that are now transferred to the New Testament life in the kingdom of God.

Sadly the passage of time and the increase in industrialization and the growth of urban community have divorced us from regarding these factors. We have either relegated them to part of the story of Israel and so it does not apply to our context today, or we have given them mythic or naïve status in the modern world.

The twin blessings renewed

However, there are many in our postmodern world who are renewing their respect of care of creation and this principle of blessing the land. One such voice is that of Norman Wirzba. He challenges us to wake up and be more consistent in our faith. He finds it ironic that Christians speak of God the Creator while showing scant regard for the creation itself. He labels this 'reconciliation deficit disorder'.[6] His thesis is that a sick land produces a sick people. He encourages us to think creatively about relocating ourselves in the land as resources for blessing and stewardship. I have explored this subject in some depth in my book *Healing Wounded History* and commend that to you, as it is not the purpose of this book to investigate this aspect in too much depth.[7]

Revivals in heart and the environment

There are a number of examples where the issue of twin blessings and holy living are being given new and fresh expressions. One of the early contributors to this growing awareness and engagement in blessing the land is the work of the Sentinel Group, who have provided anecdotal evidence of the connection between people coming to faith and the effects on the land itself. They reported in their first Transformation video, hosted by George Otis Junior, on the revival in Almalonga in Guatemala, where the revival was accompanied by a remarkable growth in crops and vegetables of a size never seen before. The Christian Broadcast Network reported on a revival in the early part of this century in the town of Toowoomba in Queensland, Australia. The report stated that following on from the revival the elders of this little village noticed that the water supply suddenly improved. Apparently it had been undrinkable for over 40 years but now the fish were returning and even the grass was growing on the riverbanks again.

What if anything are we to deduce from these stories? The first thing is to say we cannot dismiss them as so much fancy because there is a growing body of evidence, albeit anecdotal, of this phenomenon. What it affirms is the connection between the twin blessings of Genesis 1: spiritual revival brings healing not just to people and relationships but the environment itself. Chris Styles, in his blog for

Street Pastors from St Pancras Church in Chichester, says that it is as though some of the conditions of Eden are being restored. This may sound idyllic but I think he has hold of a truth that God's disposition is to bless people within their location, to experience flourishing not only in their spiritual lives but in the land that is co-beneficiary of this blessing. Consequently I think we need to take seriously our stewardship of the creation again and in our prayers to pray blessing on the land and its community that they flourish together.

An example of this for me came as a result of visiting a ranch in South Carolina owned by my friends Jean and Jonny Corbett. Embree is a 400-acre reserve with a large lake for fishing and there are also deer for hunting. The Corbetts welcome a host of people who go there for retreat and fellowship, and many times it has been used for men's groups. One day Jean and Jonny asked me if I would write and conduct a blessing prayer for the Edisto River that runs around the perimeter of their grounds. Their idea was that they wanted the location itself to be a blessing to all who came there to canoe or fish. They wanted the location to be a place of welcome from the Lord. Consequently I wrote the following blessing:

> Dear Father, Son and Holy Spirit, we bless this river to be a river of life from God. To all who drink from it, receive God's refreshing touch on your life, on your family and on your dreams: so that in drinking you drink down deep the message that God is calling you to new life in him.
>
> We bless this Edisto River with the cleanness of God's heart, so that fish may abound in it and find their way home through it; we bless this river to carry the river of God's gift of life, and take his pure love to all who come to its banks and to the oceans where it spills out its gift of blessings.
>
> We bless this river to be a reminder of the ever-present life-giving presence of God, who has come to heal all hurting hearts and who will one day pronounce his blessings and heal the whole earth.
>
> We pronounce this blessing to the praise and glory of our Lord Christ. Amen.

Interestingly enough, since pronouncing this blessing prayer on the site many others have come there to be still in the presence of God and have found it a very helpful place to be. Subsequently Jean and

Jonny have erected a cross on the site and created more space for people to come and sit on a new pier for quiet meditations. One such visitor was Mark Lawrence, the Bishop of the Diocese of South Carolina, who took a copy of the blessing prayer to use elsewhere.

New Monasticism

The last ten years have witnessed the emergence of new cluster communities with a rule of life that among other things focuses on returning to the combination of living simply on the earth, reverencing the earth and serving society with the love of Christ. One of the leaders of this monasticism is Jonathan Wilson-Hartgrove, who helped compile the 12 marks or attitudes of living that characterize these communities. Mark number nine states, 'Care for the plot of God's earth given to us along with support of our local economies.'[8] He concludes his list of 12 with this request, 'May God give us grace by the power of the Holy Spirit to discern rules for living that will help us embody these marks in our local contexts as signs of Christ's kingdom for the sake of God's world.'[9]

For Wilson-Hartgrove, the New Monasticism is a return to the twin blessings of caring for persons alongside caring for worlds. It is interesting that many in this movement look to ancient traditions to learn timeless principles for present-day encounter and mission. This is not only true for New Monastics but also for the Fresh Expressions initiatives and the new Celtic communities such as the Community of Aidan and Hilda and the Northumbria Community. It is a recognition of the neglected riches of the Church's long story and the need to invent fresh connections with them. One example I would like to focus on was the habit of our Celtic Christian ancestors when they wanted to plant new communities. The standard routine was to commit 40 days to fasting and praying for the cleansing and healing of the land. In particular Bede, in his *Ecclesiastical History of the English People*, writes about the prayers of St Cedd in preparing the ground for the new monastery of Lastingham near Pickering in Yorkshire.[10] The land was regarded as polluted by the evil deeds of men perpetrated on it, so that it had become the habitation of demons. Bede quotes from Isaiah 35 when he says that the intent of the saint was to convert the land poisoned by dragons so that it would soon blossom and flourish and rushes would grow again.[11] The blessing and healing of the land produced the location for a community of faith to flourish and made possible the restoration of the land to fruitfulness. The ancient Celtic Christians saw a dynamic interplay between creation and community flourishing. This was not a sanitization of the sympathetic magic of their pagan forebears but a practice of the age-old biblical principle of twin blessings as the context for sharing good news. It is this connection that has led to a proliferation of Christian initiatives to pray for and bless the needs of the community so that their land, produce and lives might flourish.

However, before we look at some examples of these, let us first look at another ancient tradition that may inspire us to take the ministry of blessing the land more seriously. I am speaking of the ancient rite of rogation.

Rogation Days

The Rogation Days were usually celebrated on the Monday, Tuesday and Wednesday before Ascension Day. It was essentially an outdoor activity of processions and blessing prayers focused on the stewardship of creation. The practice originated in Vienne in France in 470 after a series of natural disasters that had devastated the community. Archbishop Mamertus announced a fast and ordered that special litanies and prayers be said as the people processed around their fields, asking God's protection and blessing the crops that were about to germinate. The Latin word *rogare* means 'to ask' and comes from the fact that the Gospel set for these processions was from John 16, where Jesus tells his disciples to 'ask, and you shall receive'.

In an agricultural society, closely connected with the soil and highly vulnerable to the uncertainties of nature, it is no surprise that this idea took root quickly. The custom spread throughout Europe and over to Britain. Over time the activity developed into popular festivals celebrating the arrival of spring that were spread over a number of days. The route of the walk was around the boundaries of the parish, which was a civil as well as a religious unit, and it became popularly known as 'beating the bounds'. En route the procession would stop at various landmarks, such as a venerable tree, a pond or other noticeable landmark, where the Gospel would be read, prayers of blessing prayed and sometimes a cross fixed to the location itself. Boundaries are very important in relationships. Robert Frost, in his poem 'Mending the Wall' (1914), recounts a conversation of two neighbours meeting to talk about repairing the boundaries that separate their respective properties, and in agreeing to restore the boundary, Frost stated 'Good fences make good neighbours.' Rogationtide was an opportunity literally to mend the fences and so was focused on the need to reconcile broken relationships as well as broken boundaries. In his book *Arcadia*, Adam Nicolson quotes the seventeenth-century poet George Herbert as saying that there were four reasons to applaud the practice of Rogationtide:

1 A Blessing of God for the fruits of the field.
2 Justice in the preservation of bounds.
3 Charity in loving, walking and neighbourly accompanying one another with reconciling of differences at the time if there be any.
4 Mercie, in relieving the poor by a liberal distribution of largesse, which at the time is or ought to be used.[12]

For Herbert, there were four dimensions of a village's existence: metaphysical, legislative, personal and social. Rogation therefore became one of the public demonstrations of Christian solidarity with the needs and welfare of the community it served.

Modern applications of rogation ministry

Who can forget the horror of the outbreak of foot and mouth disease on a host of farms in this country in the early part of this century? The television showed us stark images of mountains of carcasses of cattle being burned and farms quarantined for long durations until the crisis had passed. Then came the sad tales of those famers who, in utter despair at the loss of their livelihood and feeling abandoned by those who lived safely in the cities, resorted to suicide. This so challenged my friend John Presdee, a Baptist pastor from Orpington in Kent, that he felt called by God to do something about it. He wanted to show solidarity with the farmers and he believed God was calling him to heal the affected lands. Though his church tradition was not sacramental, he was nonetheless convinced that he should go and celebrate Holy Communion and prayers of blessings with the afflicted farming families. So John set off for Cumbria in particular and began a series of visits to those farms most affected. Although greeted sometimes with scepticism he held a communion at the gates of those farms. The amazing fact is that wherever he did this, the disease rapidly vanished from the soil and the cattle were pronounced clean. Others may describe this as superstition or coincidence but John, the Baptist pastor, was applying the age-long principle of twin blessings embedded in the rogation ministry we have been examining.

Praying on wounded sites

The twenty-first century has seen an explosion in intercessory prayer initiatives focused on the needs and blessing of communities. My first encounter with this was at Warren Point near Newry in Northern Ireland. It was here that the Provisional IRA exploded a roadside bomb that killed and maimed the soldiers who were passing by. When the medics later arrived to tend to the needs of the wounded, another bomb was detonated, killing and injuring the doctors and nurses. Nearby was the Christian Renewal Centre and its leader, the Revd Cecil Kerr, led a service of remembrance and blessing on this site. One of the reasons, he later reported, for doing this was to help people connect with the location in a way that evoked the desire for healing and reconciliation and not to sink into the power and effects of the violence perpetrated there. It gave the people who lived there an opportunity to voice their feelings and also to move on. Nothing could change what had happened there but with God's healing touch we can change the way we relate to the place.

Neighbourhood blessings

In the 1970s, C. Peter Wagner and Ed Silvoso among others developed the practice of prayer-walking in the city as a means of focusing on the spiritual battles required to help further the proclamation of the gospel in those cities. The focus was usually on the spiritual powers that influenced the mindset of a community and needed to be disarmed. They had their critics, who thought such activities were not very productive, and in the course of time the practice diminished. However, a new expression of praying in the city has emerged that focuses more on blessing prayers for the city. As we have already noted, one of the better-known expressions of this has been the community of Ffald-y-Brenin in Pembrokeshire, South Wales. Based on Jesus' words in Luke 10.5, where Jesus instructed his disciples to pray for the peace of the towns they visited, Roy and Daphne Godwin, the current leaders at Ffald-y-Brenin, set about praying weekly for the blessing of their rural communities. Between them they also fostered the foundation of a number of houses of prayer with the sole purpose of being a blessing to their community.

> There is a strong tendency for Christians to criticize and judge people and behaviours we term sinful. In a local house of prayer we are going to change all that and have a heart to love and to bless, to see good and trust the Lord to deal with the bad.[13]

Following on from the National Day of Prayer held in the Wembley Arena in September 2012 there has come an initiative to promote a variety of Christian activity with the common denominator of being a blessing to the community. It is called The Neighbourhood Prayer Net and is supported by a host of Christian enterprises. Rebekah Brettle and Lyndall Bywater have produced a resource book called *Neighbours, Transform Your Street!*.[14] This contains a host of stories illustrating the challenging outcomes and projects born on the wings of blessing, and very usefully has a chapter on planning a prayer-walk of blessing.[15]

Another example of blessing on the streets is found in the work of Street Pastors. In their article on praying blessing they refer to Jeremiah 29.7, which says 'seek the peace and prosperity of the city to which I have carried you into exile. Pray to the Lord for it, because if it prospers, you too will prosper.' This connects well with Jesus' words to the disciples on mission in community that we have already read. With this in mind the Street Pastors article offers the following prayers of blessing on the community:

A blessing for a town

> Heavenly Father, we take upon ourselves the mantle of authority that Jesus delegates to us and in His Name we speak to every household in this town and surrounding area and say to you:
>
> > We bless you in the Name of the Lord. We bless your marriages that they may be strong and whole. We bless the relationships between each marriage partner that they may be loving, forgiving, merciful and strong. We bless every intergenerational

relationship within each household that there may be peace and love and understanding flowing between each one.

In Jesus' name we bless every network of wholesome and supportive friendship.

We bless your health that you may be strong and well. In Jesus' name we resist any sickness or disease which seeks to invade this town and to every person in the surrounding area we say, be well, be strong, be healthy. To any who are sick right now we say we bless you in Jesus' name with a speedy recovery.

We bless your wealth that you may have plenty to replace poverty. We bless you enough to live and enough to give. We bless the work of your hands that whatever you turn your hand to which is wholesome may be profitable. We bless every wholesome enterprise that is conducted by you that it may prosper and be successful. We bless the shops and restaurants in every good that you do.

We bless the residential homes for the elderly, that they may be secure, safe and peaceful places where those who live there may be loved and cared for in a way that maintains their dignity.

We bless preschools, schools, colleges and universities (name those within the town or those that you know the name of), that they may be secure, safe places for teachers and pupils alike.

We bless the children's capacity to learn and develop relationships and we bless their simple trust in Jesus that their trust may grow and become enriched.

We speak to the churches (name as many that you know), and we say we bless you in the Name of the Lord that the Holy Spirit and the Word of God may flow out from you in power. We bless the hearts of all who live in and work in this town and surrounding area, that the overspill of the blessings of the presence of the kingdom of God may fall upon you.[16]

Whereas we may find this blessing prayer very detailed and perhaps overlong, it nonetheless demonstrates the rogation ministry of ancient tradition revitalized in a contemporary context. I will never forget taking part in a blessing prayer that took place on one of the bridges over the gorge that divides the town of Tiverton in Devon. It took place after a series of meetings exploring the needs of reconciliation between two churches that had been joined in a united benefice. Once this work was completed it seemed appropriate for the two congregations to bless the people of the town that they too might know encouragement and reconciliation in their own lives. So almost a hundred of us stood on the bridge and used the old Celtic form of encirclement prayer. Stretching out an arm we slowly rotated in a clockwise circle, and on everything to which our hands pointed we would pronounce blessing and remind ourselves that the earth is the Lord's and everything in it! When we had finished some people came out of the shops to ask us what we were doing. They didn't seem surprised at all that the church had had problems and were glad we wanted to bless them.

There are now many resources available to hold your own contemporary rogation ministry or street blessing service and they come from a variety of sources, such as the Diocese of Worcester, the Northumbria Community and the Environmental Stewardship Commission.[17]

Conclusion

It is exciting to see old traditions being given a contemporary application and fresh expression. It is not just on the streets that these new liturgies are focused but also the blessings of homes, businesses and churches. Antony Billington demonstrates how the Old Testament book of Ruth has as one of its major themes the blessing of home and homecoming.[18]

The story begins with a parting, with Naomi urging her widowed daughters-in-law to return to their homes in Moab and effectively praying a blessing on them (1.8–9). In doing so she commits their future to God, seeking his kindness for them and praying that God will grant them the security that comes from being married rather than the vulnerability that would come with widowhood. The next blessing occurs in 2.4, as Boaz greets his harvesters with, The Lord be with you!', and they reply with, 'The Lord bless you!' Although this may be no more than a greeting (but what a greeting!), it's a lovely reminder of God's presence in the everyday, with the use of God's name to invoke his blessing in daily life and work in the meeting and leaving of friends. In his first encounter with Ruth, Boaz prays a blessing for Ruth's well-being because of her faithfulness to Naomi (2.11–12), words that are picked up again in his blessing of her in 3.10 as she dares to seek Boaz as her next of kin. Ruth 2.19–20 then records Naomi's reaction to Ruth, 'Blessed be the man' – with a prayer seeking God's blessing on Boaz. Then, after Boaz and Ruth are married, those who witness the occasion seek God for the provision of children and the building up of their household (4.11–12). When a child is born, the women bless God in thanksgiving for dealing kindly with Naomi (4.14–15). Naomi's desire for Ruth to find security in a husband's house (1.9) has come true. In a story shot through with covenant faithfulness, the blessing she sought has come about in the blessing from God of a family from whom will come king David (4.18–22), from whom will come Christ himself (Matt. 1.5).

We can conclude that the twin blessings of Genesis provide us with a template for the engagement of being a blessing and pronouncing blessings within our community and on the land itself. We are living in days of extraordinary grace, and I think one of the windows of opportunity to see that grace outpoured is in taking seriously and imaginatively the recovery of our God-given commission to bless and be a blessing.

10

Learning to pronounce blessings

'Bless – that's your job, to bless.' (1 Peter 3.9 *The Message*)

When the nation of Israel had been delivered from the threat of extinction by the Assyrians, King Hezekiah called for a national celebration and a rededicating of the nation to devotion to Yahweh. The crowning conclusion to the 14 days of festivals, songs and prayers was the blessing prayer of the priests and Levites. 'The priests and Levites stood to bless the people, and God heard them, for their prayer reached heaven, his holy dwelling place' (2 Chron. 30.27). There was a deep awareness that the pronouncing of blessings better connected them with the purposes of heaven. This is not to say that blessings render all other forms of prayer and intercessions obsolete but it does affirm the power there is in pronouncing blessings. It is this intentional form of blessing that we need to recapture in the practice of our Christian faith. Barbara Brown Taylor, in her book *An Altar in the World*, would go further and say that we need to cultivate a rhythm of blessing in our everyday awareness. She encourages us to become more in touch with the presence of God in his creation and the people around us and to pronounce proactively blessings on all that we see.

> The next time you are at the airport, try blessing the people sitting at the departure gate with you. Every one of them is dealing with something significant. See that mother trying to contain her explosive two-year-old? See that pock-faced boy with the huge belly? Even if you cannot know for sure what is going on with them, you can still give a care. They are on their way somewhere, the same way you are. They are between places too, with no more certainty than you about what will happen at the other end. Pronounce a silent blessing and pay attention to what happens in the air between you and that other person, all those other people.[1]

We have already mentioned in this book the range of blessings given in the Bible and that they were not restricted to the priestly or ministerial office.

When Rebekah left her family to become Isaac's wife her family blessed her by saying 'may you increase to thousands upon thousands; may your offspring possess the cities of their enemies' (Gen. 24.60). Melchizedek blessed Abraham for honouring God for his protection and victory and for Abraham's tithing instead of conceding to the offers of the king of Sodom to take the goods for himself (Gen. 14.8–24). When Isaac was ready to die, he pronounced his blessing on his son, Jacob (Gen. 27.28–29). When Boaz came into his harvest field he greeted his workers with the usual greeting of, 'The LORD be with you!' and their response was to say, 'The LORD bless you!' (Ruth 2.4). Naomi pronounces a blessing on Boaz when she discovers his care of Ruth and her own husband's family heritage. She proclaimed, 'The LORD bless him! . . . He has not stopped showing his kindness to the living and the dead' (Ruth 2.20). King David, after dedicating the Ark of God in Jerusalem, went home in celebration to bless his family (1 Chron. 16.43). The first time Jesus was blessed was when he was still in his mother's womb. His cousin Elizabeth, filled with the Holy Spirit, prophetically calls out to mother and unborn child, 'Blessed are you among women, and blessed be the child you will bear!' (Luke 1.42). The last time that Jesus was blessed in this way was on his way into the city of Jerusalem! The anonymous crowd greet him at the gates with the words, 'Hosanna to the Son of David! Blessed is he who comes in the name of the Lord! Hosanna in the highest heaven!' (Matt. 21.9). Here they were echoing the words of the psalmist who was extolling gratitude to God for the deliverance of Israel from their enemies: 'Blessed is he who comes in the name of the LORD. From the house of the LORD we bless you' (Ps. 118.26).

In summary we can say that the weight of evidence from Scripture is that blessing is something open to all and that it is a normal resource applied to a host of everyday circumstances. In addition, if we take seriously the description of Christians as the new priesthood of all believers, then the challenge is for us to put this lost ministry back into normal usage in our lives.

Barbara Brown Taylor recounts the following episode in her life that brought the reality and impact of blessing afresh to her heart.

> My father died after a small seizure caused by his advanced brain cancer knocked him for a loop two weeks before Christmas. After the seizure was over and the ambulance had taken him to the hospital, my mother and I followed in my car. Soon his small cubicle in the emergency room was full of my sisters, their sons, and our husbands, all crowded on a white bench set against the wall.
>
> While we were doing this, I noticed my husband get up and go over to my father, leaning down to say something in his ear. He knelt down on the linoleum floor by my father's bed and fitted his head underneath my father's bony hand. As I watched, Ed reached up and put one of his big hands on top of my father's hand to make sure it did not slip off. Then he held still while my father's lips moved. After he stood up, he leaned over to say something else in my father's ear.
>
> 'What was that?' I asked when he came back to slump beside me again.
>
> 'I asked him to bless me,' Ed said. 'I asked him to give me his blessing.'[2]

She went on to explain that this kind of blessing prayer was called a benediction. It comes at the end of something, to send people on their way. As such it gave her a new conviction on the importance and access to blessing that is open to us all.

> All I am saying is that anyone can do this. Anyone can ask and anyone can bless, whether anyone has authorized you to do it or not. All I am saying is that the world needs you to do this, because there is a real shortage of people willing to kneel wherever they are and recognize the holiness holding its sometimes bony, often tender, always life-giving hand above their heads. That we are able to bless one another at all is evidence that we have been blessed, whether we can remember when or not. That we are willing to bless one another is miracle enough to stagger the very stars.[3]

In his home blog, Daniel Fusco emphasizes this very point when he states that he longs for pastors to bless their congregations publicly and often, in Jesus' name; for husbands to share the benediction with their wives and wives with their husbands; for parents to share it with their children; for brothers to bless their sisters and sisters their brothers; for employers to bless their employees and employees their employers; for blessing to be proclaimed across party, denominational and socio-economic lines, across international boundaries and to the ends of the earth.[4]

Building blocks for pronouncing blessings

The following are some of the basic steps to help us prepare the blessings we want to declare over another. Naturally it is preferable to do this with the person we are blessing, but it does need to be affirmed that we can also bless when the other is absent. This is especially applicable to sons, daughters and grandchildren who are far away from us, for good reasons and bad. Just as we pray and intercede for our children we see, we can also bless those we do not see but hold dear in our hearts.

Prepare yourself

When blessing another it is to be done from a position of humility and gratitude to God for all the good things he has done in our lives. We do not bless another from a position of superiority but from the servant heart of Jesus. In preparing ourselves we also need to connect with the fact that authority to do so is from God and not our own experience or achievements. It would be good, therefore, to begin by thanking God for his blessings and stating that it is our desire to pass those blessings on for others to share. Remember the confession of Elizabeth as she blessed Mary and Jesus: 'Why am I so favoured?' (Luke 1.43). Before blessing others she herself had just been blessed with the filling of the Holy Spirit.

In his book *Blessing Your Children*, Jack Hayford suggests the following prayer to be made especially when you are preparing to bless your own children:

> Father, I am astounded . . . that You would confer upon me the overwhelming privilege of being Your representative in both announcing and pronouncing Your blessing upon a child. As I receive this truth . . . I make this declaration:
>
> You are my God, and it is Your almighty throne I honor in this action of blessing children. I denounce any notion that my words

are the source of the power in this blessing, but I also deny any idea that suggests my words are unimportant in this dramatic transaction. The fact that You make me Your middleman, reaching to heaven – to Your throne and then to a child, who is Your created wonder and given to me to love and serve – is an awesome wonder in my sight. And so I ask You to help me minister blessings always with wisdom, always with faith and always with that gentle grace that will cause the children in my life to know by that blessing how beloved they are by You and by me. In Your holy name. Amen.[5]

Decide whom to bless – building, church, company

Sometimes God lays on our heart someone who needs our blessing prayers. However, it is more common that we carry concerns and cares for various people, and alongside our intercessions for them we might want to bless them. At others time we may experience those occasional inner nudges for perfect strangers on the street or friends we have at work. I have learnt to pray silent blessings on them as soon as I get those nudges. We have already seen that there is a place for proactive blessings for our neighbours and we make this a regular part of our church's ministry whether in church meetings or while prayer-walking in the streets.

If you live in an agricultural or rural community you may want to construct a modern rogation blessing for the land and farmers in your area. It might be a good idea to involve the community in the service you put together so that you can come on their land to ask God to bless the soil that it produces the desired harvest of crops. You may want to bless the health of both the farmers and their livestock. There are plenty of resources available and I would point you to the website of Worcester Diocese, who have produced a number of suggestions on how to do this and provided a selection of blessing prayers.

Many people want to bless their church life, especially if it is in need of healing or renewal of life. You may like to think of offering special blessing prayers on the ministers and their families or all the leaders of the church community. I have written a liturgy called 'The Christian Day of Atonement' that offers some suggestions for blessing of the places of ministry within the church.[6]

Deciding what to say

Blessings are not wishful thinking, nor are they our hopes couched in prayer. It is good practice to ask the following questions in order to arrive at a blessing we can say with faith and confidence:

- What is on my heart for that person?
- What do I believe God wants to do for this person?
- As a parent blessing a son or daughter or another close relative, what do I believe they need in order to flourish as the person God has called them to be?
- As a parent you are the only one who can give the father or mother blessing to your children, so ask yourself, 'What do I want my son or daughter to receive from me that tells them I love and celebrate them?' You could begin your blessing with the words, 'My son or daughter, I bless you with knowing that I love, honour and celebrate you . . .'
- If you are blessing a part of creation such as the ground, a river or cattle and crops, focus on what good outcomes you would want God to bring from them. The same principle applies if you are blessing your workplace and workforce.
- You may want to bless your ministers, so think of what you would want God to enrich in their service for Christ.[7]

Make sure that when you bless that you are as specific as you need to be and avoid too many distracting words.

Another basic element in many of the biblical blessings is the request for flourishing and increase of life. Consider the following examples:

1. Adam and Eve: 'And God blessed them saying, "Be fruitful and multiply"' (Gen. 1.22 NKJV).
2. Abraham: 'Blessing I will bless you, and multiplying I will multiply your descendants as the stars of heaven and as the sand which is on the seashore' (Gen. 22.17 NKJV).
3. Paul blessing the church at Thessalonica: 'the Lord make you increase and abound in love to one another and to all, just as we do to you' (1 Thess. 3.12 NKJV).

Show your dependence on God

When Jacob blessed the sons of Joseph he included words that said that he was in a place to do this because his life depended on God's support and activity. 'May the God before whom my fathers Abraham and Isaac walked faithfully, the God who has been my shepherd all my life to this day, the Angel who has delivered me from all harm – may he bless these boys' (Gen. 48.15–16). When we bless others it is good to include reference and praise to the God who has been our faithful saviour – it demonstrates that we are in the position to bless because of God and not because of our own strength or achievements. It also indicates that we are looking to God to bring about the blessings we say.

Pronounce your blessing

It is apparent in Scripture that blessings were pronounced and not requested. Although the word 'may' occurs before many of the blessings in the Bible, it refers to a desire for God to act and make real that blessing. Such pronouncing also focuses us on our need to exercise faith and to speak out boldly and in trust of God. It also underlines our dependency and expectation for God to determine the outcome of our blessing pronouncements.

Speaking to the person

It is preferable to pronounce your blessing on a person when he or she is with you. This helps create openness to God and expectancy in God from the recipient of the blessing. As you bless, always see that your demeanour conveys the spirit and heart of our loving, living God. He not only wants to bless the person but has also called you and me to accept the responsibility for directly *inviting* that blessing.

The *expression* on your face, the *tone* with which you speak, the *touch* of your hand placed on the person's head or shoulder, and the *time* and *timing* of your blessing should be appropriate to the moment and contribute to the person's sense of being loved because they are being blessed.

Speaking to the person when they are absent

It is just as important and effective to pronounce blessings on those who are not present. This is especially true if there has been a breakdown in relationship and you want to reach out to the person to begin a healing and restoring process. I would also encourage you to make personal contact as a follow-through action.

When you bless those who are absent I encourage you to do so as if they were just across the street from you (I recounted a personal instance of this in Chapter 7). Call out your blessing on them as if in faith you are endeavouring to catch their attention and bring them home to your heart. Here are some examples:

> 'Jack! I bless you with my father's love. I bless you with knowing just how much God loves you!'
>
> 'Jane! I bless you with my mother's love. I bless you with knowing how lovely you are!'

Follow through with appropriate action

It is important to reflect on what is a good way to follow through from our intentional blessings with practical actions that build on them. Our blessings are a commitment to live a life that is a blessing to others. If you have pronounced blessings on your children, for example, think of how you can build on those pronouncements. If you have blessed children with whom relationship has been damaged or broken, think of writing a letter to develop the theme of your blessing and include an apology if necessary. I am always challenged when I think of the Parable of the Prodigal Son (Luke 15.11–31): the father was looking out for his son to return and, when he did, celebrated him rather than pointing out the sins he had committed or the heartache he had caused.

Conclusion

Be the people that bless!

11

Blessing prayers for various occasions

Blessing for spiritual growth

I bless you with knowing the joy of the Lord that is your strength.
I bless you with knowing joy in his faithfulness in profound and life-giving ways.
I bless you with remembering times when he showed you his faithfulness.
I bless you with enlarging your spirit to know profoundly and deeply that your Father is pleased with you.
I bless you with receiving the truth of your identity, legitimacy and birthright.
I bless you with knowing who you are in your Father's eyes and in drinking deeply of the joy that he has in who you are.

(Sylvia Gunter)[1]

A non-traditional blessing

May God bless you with **discontent** with easy answers, half-truths, superficial relationships, so that you will live from deep within your heart.
May God bless you with **anger** at injustice, oppression, abuse, and exploitation of people, so that you will work for justice, equality, and peace.
May God bless you with **tears** to shed for those who suffer from pain, rejection, starvation and war, so that you will reach out your hand to comfort them and to change their pain to joy.
May God bless you with the **foolishness** to think you can make a difference in this world, so that you will do the things which others tell you cannot be done.

If you have the courage to accept these blessings, then God will also bless you with

happiness – because you will know that you have made life better for others.
inner peace – because you will have worked to secure an outer peace for others.
laughter – because your heart will be light.
faithful friends – because they will recognize your worth as a person.

These blessings are yours – not for the asking, but for the giving – from One who wants to be your companion, our God, who lives and reigns, forever and ever. Amen.

(Sr Ruth Fox OSB)[2]

God, who from the death of sin raised you to new life in Christ, keep you from falling and set you in the presence of his glory; and the blessing of God almighty, the Father, the Son, and the Holy Spirit, be among you and remain with you always.

(*Common Worship*)[3]

Blessing for a town

We stand in the mighty name of Jesus and bless you [name of town], that you might prosper under the mighty hand of God.

We bless you that justice and righteousness might take their proper place within your boundaries.

We bless you that the favour of the Lord might rest upon you and give you peace.

We bless you that the Father's compassion might fall upon your people.

We bless your poor that they might be lifted up.

We bless you that the knowledge of Jesus might come in among you like a flood.

We bless the people of God in [name of town] that they might rise up with servant authority and become a people of blessing.

We bless you that the joy of the Lord might be your strength. Amen.

(Worldwide Mission Fellowship)[4]

In the Name of Jesus I speak out to you, my street and neighbourhood, that God loves you and cares for you.

I bless you that a spirit of salvation might come upon you, that the Spirit of Truth might reveal Jesus.

I bless you that you might prosper in body, soul and spirit and that you might always have enough.

I bless you that your hearts might be softened towards one another and to Jesus. Amen.

(Adapted from a prayer by Daphne Godwin)

Blessing for a workplace

Thankfulness: Bless the Lord O my soul and forget not all his benefits. We bless you, Lord, for your gift of work – for the opportunity to co-labour with you and to provide for our families and communities.

Output: We bless the creativity and skills you have given, which enable us to make goods and deliver services that others need.

Relationships: We bless every contact with another person, be they colleague, customer or supplier. We bless those we meet, speak to or email that they may experience something of your love through us.

Resources: We bless the use and stewardship of all resources available in our organizations.

Organization: We bless the organizations for which we work; we bless them as employers and pray that job opportunities may multiply through them. We bless the management decisions to reflect kingdom values.

Culture: We bless the culture of our organization. May it be a context for human flourishing – a place where people feel valued.

(The London Institute for Contemporary Christianity)[5]

Blessing of soil

God, you have created us and given us this soil. The soil serves as the medium for the seed to grow, it cleans water, it regulates climate. It provides warmth, nourishment and support so that new life may emerge. Bless this soil that it may feed and nourish the seed. Bless those who work this soil and harvest they produce.

(Rural Church Support Network for Yorkshire and The Humber)[6]

Blessing of water

God, this water is your creation. Water gives sustenance and nourishment to the soil and the seed. Bless the soil and the seed with gentle rain. Bless this water. Let it come as rain at the right time, in the proper amount so that the seed may flourish and grow. In your mercy send us favourable weather so that the harvest will be bountiful. Amen.

(Rural Church Support Network for Yorkshire and The Humber)[7]

Blessing of land and life

May the blessing of light be on you – light without and light within.
May the blessed sunlight shine on you like a great peat fire,
so that stranger and friend may come and warm himself at it.
And may light shine out of the two eyes of you,
like a candle set in the window of a house,
bidding the wanderer come in out of the storm.
And may the blessing of the rain be on you,
may it beat upon your Spirit and wash it fair and clean,
and leave there a shining pool where the blue of Heaven shines,
and sometimes a star.
And may the blessing of the earth be on you,
soft under your feet as you pass along the roads,
soft under you as you lie out on it, tired at the end of day;
and may it rest easy over you when, at last, you lie out under it.
May it rest so lightly over you that your soul may be out from
under it quickly; up and off and on its way to God.
And now may the Lord bless you, and bless you kindly. Amen.

(Scottish blessing)[8]

In the strong name of Jesus
We bless all that is living,
And recognize in all that lives

The reflection of the word who said,
'Let there be life,'
and it lives. (The Blessing of Ninian, *Celtic Daily Prayer*)[9]

House and home blessings

God the Father Almighty, bless and sanctify this home, those who live in it and everything that is in it.

Be so kind as to fill this home with all good things and grant those who live here the abundance of blessings from heaven and substance of life from the richness of the earth. Direct the longings of their prayer to the fruits of your mercy.

Be so kind as to bless and sanctify this home at our coming in, just as you blessed the home of Abraham, Isaac and Jacob. May your angels of light live within the walls of this house and guard it and all who live in it through Jesus Christ our Lord. Amen.

(Praesidium of Warriors of St Michael, adapted)[10]

God bless the corners of this house and all the lintel blessed,
And bless the hearth and bless the board and bless each place of rest,
And bless each door that opens wide to strangers as to kin,
And bless each crystal window pane that lets the starlight in,
And bless the rooftree overhead and every sturdy wall.
The peace of man. The peace of God. With peace and love for all. (Irish blessing)[11]

Blessings for good endings

Therefore, as the times of life go by you,
Deep peace of the ever-present king be yours.
When you remember all those unfinished things;
Deep surrender to the Easter Christ be yours.
When the moment of letting go is yours to give,
Deep holding of heaven's shining Lord be yours.
When there is nothing else to say or to be done,
Deep speech of the one who says 'Come up here,
And see what must be,'
Be yours. Amen. (Russ Parker)[12]

Blessing of a marriage

May God be with you and bless you.
May you see your children's children.
May you be poor in misfortune.
Rich in blessings.
May you know nothing but happiness.
From this day forward. (Irish marriage blessing)[13]

May your home be filled with laughter and the warm embrace of a summer day. May you find peacefulness and beauty, challenge, and satisfaction, humour and insight, healing and renewal, love and wisdom, as in a quiet heart. May you always feel that what you have is enough. Amen. (Anonymous)[14]

Blessings for children

Dearest Father in Heaven,
Bless this child and bless this day
Of new beginnings.
Smile upon this child
And surround this child, Lord,
With the soft mantle of your love.
Teach this child to follow in your footsteps,
And to live life in the ways of
Love, faith, hope and charity.

(A Gaelic Christening Blessing)[15]

My son, I bless you with my father's love that you will grow into the man God wants you to be. I bless you with knowing just how much we honour and celebrate the fact that you are our son. I bless you with more of God's father heart of grace and power in your life that you will flourish in all your hopes and walk by faith as you journey through this life.

My daughter, I bless you with my mother's love that you will grow into the woman that God wants you to be. I bless you with knowing how lovely and wonderful you are and I celebrate that you are my daughter. I bless you with knowing how much God cares for you and rejoices over you. I bless you that your life will flourish in the love of God. (Russ Parker)

Blessing for health professionals

We bless all doctors and nurses that God would use their skills to bring healing to the sick and needy. We bless them with the refreshing touch of God so that they will be renewed and encouraged as they serve in an often busy and demanding environment. We bless their families and homes with the peace of Christ. We bless them with insight to see the presence of God in all that they do. Amen. (Russ Parker)

Blessings for a journey

May the road rise up to meet you,
May the wind always be at your back,
May the sunshine warm your face,
And rains fall soft upon your fields.
And until we meet again,
May God hold you in the palm of His hand.

(Old Irish Blessing)[16]

Appendix
A liturgy for receiving the father and mother blessings[1]

Introduction

From the moment of conception and throughout the formative years of childhood, the love and care of our mother and father play a critical role in our development. Unfortunately, in our fallen humanity, there are no perfect parents. Subsequently, many people carry wounds or voids they incurred early in life from one or both of their parents, such as unmet needs, absence, neglect, harsh words or abusive behaviour. Nevertheless, through the power of the Holy Spirit, the Lord can go back and bring healing to these wounds with his perfect love. In an atmosphere of prayer, it is often quite powerful to have prayer ministers stand in the place of earthly parents to offer a loving hug and any words of affirmation the Lord would like to speak to this person. Below we have included a sample prayer that can be prayed over an individual or group in the context of a mother or father blessing. These prayers are intended to serve as an example and we always suggest that anyone leading these prayers be sensitive to the direction of the Holy Spirit and modify them in any way he would lead.

Preparing your team

It would be advisable to give your team some basic teaching on the father heart of God. Choose people who have a servant heart.

Instruct your ministry team to listen to God for words of blessing for each person who comes. It is helpful to ask yourself, 'As a mother or father, what would I wish God to give to my own son or daughter?' Make that the blessing you pray over the person whom you are blessing.

If they are not sure what to say in blessing prayer then encourage them to use the Aaronic blessing in Numbers 6.24–26.

People can be very vulnerable during encounters like this, so teach the team to resist the temptation to be controlling or too directive.

If members of the team believe that God is giving them a prophecy or word of knowledge when they offer the father or mother blessing, encourage them to make such insightful gifts into a blessing pronouncement. For example, if the revelation given is about some wound that needs to be healed then this could become: 'And I bless to you the healing of [whatever the particular issue is]'.

Encourage the team to keep the focus on blessing and not to stray into preaching or exhortation.

When they are called forward, instruct the team to stand in a line facing the congregation with some space between each of them to allow for some level of privacy for each person coming forward.

Preparing the reader

Pray that the Lord make you sensitive to the congregation and that where appropriate you may adapt the material as fits the circumstances.

Pray silently before beginning that the Lord make you a channel of God's healing grace.

Read the father or mother blessing prayer slowly but not too slowly.

Do not put any undue stress on any of the words spoken; let the Holy Spirit use them as God wills.

When you have finished, allow for a brief silence and then say to the congregation:

> If you wish to receive the father's/mother's blessing then please, when you are ready, do come forward to one of the team who is available for you. If there are more people waiting ahead of you then please wait your turn in silence.
>
> While people are coming forward for blessing prayer the rest of us will support you in prayer and worship.

Preparing the congregation

Before inviting people to come forward to receive the father or mother embrace and blessing, read to them the words of the father or mother blessing or both. Read thoughtfully and be free to adapt the material as you think appropriate.

When you have finished reading, explain to the congregation that you are first inviting to the front those who are standing in for our fathers or mothers. Then invite each person who wants to receive the father or mother blessing to come and stand with one of the ministry people who are available to pray blessing prayer with them.

It might be appropriate to keep silence during this time or to have some gentle worship songs to hold the moment.

When everyone has been blessed, close the time of ministry with a prayer in which the focus is trusting God to help everyone take to heart the blessings they have received.

A father's blessing prayer

A father's role is to protect, to provide, to bless, and to establish his children's identity. Maybe your father did that for you; maybe he didn't. Perhaps he abandoned you or abused you sexually, physically, verbally or emotionally.

Maybe he died before you were ready, or left you for some other reason. Maybe he made you his pet, delighting in you so much that you haven't been able to break away to be your own person. Perhaps he was distant, removed and showed no interest in you. Perhaps he terrified you with his anger and rage.

Perhaps he made you the scapegoat for all his troubles, so that you suffered for things other people did to him. Perhaps he blamed you for things that were not your fault at all.

Maybe he worked too much or played too hard and never spent time with you and so didn't join in with your games, dance recitals, birthdays and achievements.

Maybe he spent too much time with you, forcing you to become the athlete, student, doctor or lawyer you never wanted to be. Perhaps he left you in the care of hurtful, dangerous people. Maybe he didn't see or believe you when you went to him for help.

Perhaps he was just too preoccupied with himself to see anything you wanted or needed then.

I hope you are willing to hear the words of a broken father speaking to you. Please close your eyes for a few minutes.

I realize I am not your father, but please allow me to stand in for him, and in the place of your father who may, or may not, have said any of these things. Please allow yourself to hear these words:

I ask your heavenly Father to richly bless you in all the places I failed to bless you.

I ask the Lord Jesus Christ by the power of his cross and blood to set you free now from any harsh or cruel words that I said, especially the ones you keep remembering over and over. I am so sorry.

I ask the Lord to set you free from heart injuries you sustained from me or from others in whose care I placed you.

I ask the Holy Spirit to set you free from heartache, disappointments, dreads, grief or rage you cannot resolve.

I'm so sorry for any other struggles I may have caused you. May you be healed from being ignored by me or overindulged by me.

If I ever made you feel less than or not good enough I am deeply sorry and ask you to please forgive me.

May the Lord set you free from working so hard to please me when nothing ever would. May the Lord set you free from trying to get from me what I never had to give you. I'm so sorry.

May the Lord set you free from blaming me for failing you not because I need that, but so you can be free to grow, receive and to achieve. May you be creative in ways you have not yet imagined. May the Lord give you all the things I was unable or unwilling to give you.

May the Lord guide you in ways I never could and grant you peace. May the Lord free you from the effects of my addictions, my anxieties and my anger.

May the Lord free you from feeling that you have to always be perfect or that you have to be what I expected you to be. I pray that God will help you to see that the hurt and pain I caused you came from my own childhood. It limited me, and I am so sorry if it has limited you.

I pray that God will remove from you any belief that you were not wanted or loved.

I pray that the Lord will release you from any unhealthy bond that you may have with me. I want you to keep all of the good that came from me, and give what you do not need to carry to God.

[My beloved son, my precious daughter,] I love you. I am so proud of you. I am so glad you were born. I am so thankful that you are here. God your heavenly Father cause your life to flourish and be fulfilled in his healing grace.

A mother's blessing prayer

A mother's assignment is to nurture, love, tend, treasure and teach her children. Maybe your mother was wonderful; maybe she wasn't. Perhaps she abandoned you or abused you sexually, physically, verbally or emotionally.

Maybe she died before you were ready, or left you for some other reason. Maybe she made you her idol, delighting in you so much that you haven't been able to break away to be your own person.

Perhaps she made you the scapegoat for all her troubles, so that you suffered for things other people did to her that frightened, hurt or angered her.

Maybe she came between you and your father or continually forced you to choose sides.

Maybe she placed you between herself and her husband; maybe she didn't protect you from him.

Perhaps she blamed you for things that were not your fault at all. Maybe she insisted that you 'mother' her instead of her 'mothering' you. Maybe you felt important about that but did not realize you were becoming trapped and overwhelmed by the responsibility it brought.

Perhaps she left you in the care of hurtful, dangerous people. Maybe she didn't see or believe you when you went to her for help. Perhaps she was just too busy to see anything you wanted or needed then.

If you are willing to hear the words of a wounded mother speaking to you, please close your eyes for a few minutes.

I realize I am not your mother, but please allow me to stand in for her and in the place of your mother who may, or may not, have said any of these things. Please allow yourself to hear these words:

I ask the Lord Jesus Christ to set you free now from any harsh or cruel words that I said, especially the ones you keep remembering over and over. I am so sorry.

The Lord set you free from heart injuries you sustained from me or from others in whose care I placed you. The Holy Spirit set you free from heartache, disappointments, dreads, grief or rage you cannot resolve. May you be healed from being ignored or smothered by me.

If I ever made you feel less than or not good enough, I am deeply sorry and ask you to please forgive me. May the Lord set you free from working so hard to please me when nothing ever would. May the Lord set you free from trying to get from me what I never had to give to you. I am so sorry.

May the Lord set you free from blaming me for failing you, not because I need that, but so you can be free to grow, receive and achieve and be creative in ways you have not yet imagined.

May the Lord give you all the things I was unable or unwilling to give you. May the Lord guide you in ways I never could and grant you peace. May the Lord free you from any of my grief, fear, terror, anger, dread and expectations you are still trying to live up to.

May the Lord free you from feeling that you have always to be perfect. I pray that God will help you to see that the hurt and pain I caused you came from my own childhood. It limited me, and I am so sorry if it has limited you.

I pray that God will remove from you any belief that you were not wanted or loved.

Please forgive me for not nurturing you. I pray that the Lord will release you from any unhealthy bond that you may have with me. I want you to keep all of the good that came from me and give the rest to God.

[My daughter, my son,] I love you. I am so proud of you. I am so glad you were born and that you are here among us.

Be released now to be the person that God created you to be. Be free, my love, and live! God, your loving father and mother, cause your life to flourish and be fulfilled in his healing grace.

Notes

Introduction

1 Roy Godwin and Dave Roberts, *The Grace Outpouring: Blessing Others Through Prayer* (Eastbourne: David C. Cook/Kingsway, 2008).
2 Godwin and Roberts, *Grace Outpouring*, p. 17.

1 Words of blessing

1 Mike Harding, *Seed Truths: From Genesis to Revelation* (Apache Junction, AZ: Love Gospel Church, 2012), available as Kindle book or see <www.lovegospelchurch.com/seed-truths-from-genesis-to-revelations>.
2 *Theological Wordbook of the Old Testament*, ed. R. Laird Harris, vol. 1 (Chicago, IL: Moody Press, 1980), p. 132.
3 *Theological Dictionary of the New Testament*, ed. Gerhard Kittel, vol. 2 (Grand Rapids, MI: Eerdmans, 1964, repr. 1995), p. 757.

2 Blessings begin at home

1 C. F. Keil and F. Delitzsch, *1 & 2 Kings, 1 & 2 Chronicles*, Commentary on the Old Testament, vol. 3 (Peabody, MA: Hendrickson, 1989), p. 349.
2 Luciano C. Chianeque and Samuel Ngewa, in *Africa Bible Commentary*, ed. Tokunboh Adeyemo (Grand Rapids, MI: Zondervan, 2006), p. 254.
3 The curses are listed in Deuteronomy 27.15–26; 28.16–19. The blessings are listed in Deuteronomy 28.3–6.
4 *Theological Dictionary of the New Testament*, ed. Gerhard Kittel, vol. 2 (Grand Rapids, MI: Eerdmans, 1964, repr. 1995), p. 755.
5 Tracey R. Rich, 'Judaism 101', <www.jefaq.org>.
6 Jewish practice: meal hand-washing, <www.chabad.org/library/article_cdo/AID/607403/ShowFeedback/true>.
7 Michael Mayne, *This Sunrise of Wonder* (London: Darton, Longman & Todd, 2008), p. 88.
8 John J. Parsons, <www.hebrew4christians.com/Blessings/Special_Events/Seeing_a_King/seeing_a_king.html>. Another example of this can be found in Luke 7.16, the incident of the raising to life of the son of the widow of Nain.
9 William Barclay, *The Gospel of Mark*, Daily Study Bible (Edinburgh: St Andrew Press, 1986), p. 339.

10 Darrell L. Bock, *Luke*, IVP New Testament Commentary (Downers Grove, IL: IVP, 1994), p. 385. Other fellowship meals he lists are Luke 24.41–43; Acts 1.4; 10.41. Compare also John 21.9–15.

11 Augustine, 'Ep. ad Januarium', liv, i, mentioned in Roy Lawrence, *The King is Among Us: Why Jesus' Ascension Matters* (Bletchley: Scripture Union, 2004), p. 12.

12 Lawrence, *The King is Among Us*, p. 63.

13 The Northumbria Community website is <www.northumbriacommunity.org> and their email address is office@northumbriacommunity.org. The Community of Aidan and Hilda's website is <www.aidanandhilda.org> and their email address is <admin@aidanandhilda.org.uk>.

14 Ian C. Bradley, *Colonies of Heaven: Celtic Models for Today's Church*, (London: Darton, Longman & Todd, 2000), p. 58.

15 Alexander Carmichael, *Carmina Gadelica*, trans. by and as G. R. D. McLean (ed.), *Poems of the Western Highlanders* (London: SPCK, 1961).

16 McLean (ed.), *Poems of the Western Highlanders*, p. xxix.

17 Bradley, *Colonies of Heaven*, p. 61.

18 Oliver Davies and Fiona Bowie, *Celtic Christian Spirituality* (London: SPCK, 1995), pp. 41–2.

19 Bradley, *Colonies of Heaven*, pp. 80–1.

20 McLean (ed.), *Poems of the Western Highlanders*, pp. 257–8. Used by permission of SPCK.

3 The Aaronic blessing prayer

1 Roy Gane, *Leviticus, Numbers*, NIV Application Commentary (Grand Rapids, MI: Zondervan, 2004), p. 471.

2 Gane, *Leviticus, Numbers*, p. 471.

3 Norman H. Snaith, *Leviticus and Numbers*, New Century Bible Commentary (London: Nelson, 1967), p. 131.

4 Snaith, *Leviticus and Numbers*, p. 131.

5 N. Hillyer et al. (eds), *The Illustrated Bible Dictionary*, vol. 1 (Leicester: IVP, 1980), p. 496.

6 Hillyer et al. (eds), *Illustrated Bible Dictionary*, p. 539.

7 Leviticus lists a number of warnings in which God will set his face against those who eat blood (17.10); who sacrifice their children to the god Molech (20.3); who consult with mediums and spiritists (20.5–6) or who basically fail to keep God's commandments (26.17).

8 Similar exhortations to God can be found in Psalms 67.1; 80.3, 7, 19; 119.135.

9 Hillyer et al. (eds), *Illustrated Bible Dictionary*, p. 542.

10 Gane, *Leviticus, Numbers*, p. 541.

11 W. H. Bellinger, *The New International Biblical Commentary: Leviticus, Numbers* (Peabody, MA: Hendrickson, 2001), p. 202.

12 Jeff A. Benner, 'The Aaronic Blessing', <www.ancient-hebrew.org/12_blessing.html>.
13 Benner, 'Aaronic Blessing'.

4 The blessed state: Jesus and Beatitude blessings

1 Tom Wright, *Matthew for Everyone* (London: SPCK, 2002), p. 36, emphasis in original.
2 William Barclay, *The Gospel of Matthew*, vol. 1, Daily Study Bible (Edinburgh: St Andrew Press, 1972), p. 83.
3 Barclay, *Gospel of Matthew*, p. 84.
4 *The Apostolic Fathers*, vol. 1, part 2, ed. and trans. J. B. Lightfoot (Peabody, MA: Hendrickson, 1989), p. 453.
5 Stanley Hauerwas, *Matthew*, SCM Theological Commentary on the Bible (London: SCM Press, 2006), p. 60.
6 Dietrich Bonhoeffer, *Ethics*, trans. Reinhard Krauss, Charles West and Douglas C. Scott (Minneapolis, MN: Fortress Press, 2005), p. 231.
7 Hauerwas, *Matthew*, p. 61.
8 Dale Allison, *Studies in Matthew: Interpretations Past and Present* (Grand Rapids, MI: Baker, 200), p. 150.
9 William Barclay, *Gospel of Matthew*, vol. 1, rev. edn (Edinburgh: St Andrew Press, 2001), italics in original.
10 Wright, *Matthew for Everyone*, p. 38.
11 'Count Your Blessings' by Johnson Oatman Jr, in *Songs For Young People*, ed. Edwin Excell (Chicago, IL: Curtis & Jennings, 1897), no. 34.

5 Expecting blessings

1 For a further discussion of this subject see the chapter 'Land as Gift and Sacrament' in my book *Healing Wounded History: Reconciling Peoples and Healing Places* (London: Darton, Longman & Todd, 2001; SPCK, 2012). You may also wish to read the groundbreaking thesis of Walter Brueggemann, *The Land* (London: SPCK, 1978).
2 This theme of being blessed because we are doers of the word is also to be found in John 13.17, where Jesus sets an example to his disciples of what it is to serve by washing their feet. Cf. Luke 11.28.
3 The Covenant Prayer from the *Methodist Worship Book*, © 1999 Trustees for Methodist Church Purposes.
4 Yoilah Yilpet, 'Malachi', in *Africa Bible Commentary*, ed. Tokunboh Adeyemo, rev. edn (Grand Rapids, MI: Zondervan, 2010), p. 1097.
5 Donald Coggan, *Psalms 73–150*, The People's Bible Commentary (Oxford: Bible Reading Fellowship, 1999), p. 148.
6 C. F. Keil and F. Delitzsch, *Psalms*, Commentary on the Old Testament, vol. 5 (Peabody, MA: Hendrickson, 1989), p. 317.

7 Cyril Okorocha, 'Psalms', in *Africa Bible Commentary*, ed. Tokunboh Adeyemo, rev. edn (Grand Rapids, MI: Zondervan, 2010), p. 735.
8 Okorocha, 'Psalms', p. 735.
9 Thomas Ken, *Manual of Prayers for the Use of the Scholars of Winchester College*, 1674.

6 Wrestling for blessing

1 *The Complete Jewish Bible*, trans. David H. Stern (Clarksville, MD: Jewish New Testament Publications, 1998), p. 25.
2 William Gesenius, trans. Edward Robinson, *A Hebrew and English Lexicon of the Old Testament* (Oxford: Clarendon Press, 1977), p. 954.
3 *Theological Dictionary of the New Testament*, ed. Gerhard Kittel, vol. 7 (Grand Rapids, MI: Eerdmans, 1964, repr. 1995), p. 402.
4 *Theological Dictionary of the Old Testament*, ed. G. Johannes Botterweck, Helmer Ringgren and Heinz-Josef Fabry, vol. 11 (Grand Rapids, MI: Eerdmans, 1974), p. 279.
5 For further exploration into the subject of healing the legacies of family history you might like to read Kenneth McAll, *Healing the Family Tree* (London: SPCK, 2012).
6 C. F. Keil and F. Delitzsch, *The Pentateuch*, Commentary on the Old Testament, vol. 1 (Peabody, MA: Hendrickson, 1989), p. 268.
7 Keil and Delitzsch, *Pentateuch*, p. 269.
8 William E. Arp, 'The Prayer of Jabez: The Bible and the Book', *Journal of Ministry and Theology*, vol. 6, no. 2, 2002, p. 29. For other examples in the Old Testament of names connecting to experience and expectations consider Genesis 4.25 (birth of Seth); 19.37f. (birth of Moab); 29.32, 33, 35 (births of Reuben, Simeon and Judah); 30.6, 8 (births of Dan and Naphtali).
9 J. Barton Page, 'Evil,' *New Bible Dictionary* (Grand Rapids, MI: Eerdmans, 1978), p. 400.
10 Bruce Wilkinson, *The Prayer of Jabez: Breaking Through to the Blessed Life* (Colorado Springs, CO: Multnomah, 2000), p. 63.
11 Wilkinson, *Prayer of Jabez*, p. 70.
12 Phil Moore, *Straight to the Heart of Genesis* (Oxford: Monarch Books, 2010), p. 197 (italics in original).
13 Charles Haddon Spurgeon, mentioned in the Bible Bulletin Board by Tony Capoccia, <www.bible.bb.com>.
14 Arp, 'Prayer of Jabez', p. 9.
15 For a fascinating development of the relationship to covenant faith and health, see S. I. McMillen, *None of These Diseases* (Westwood, NJ: Revell, 1963).
16 John E. Hartley, *The Book of Job* (Grand Rapids, MI: Eerdmans, 1988), p. 542.

17 Wilkinson, *Prayer of Jabez*, p. 30.
18 Wilkinson, *Prayer of Jabez*, pp. 34, 35.
19 Moore, *Straight to the Heart of Genesis*, p. 197.

7 The father's blessing

1 Aaron Fruh, *The Forgotten Blessing: Ancient Words that Heal Generational Wounds* (Grand Rapids, MI: Chosen Books, 2006), p. 117.
2 Sylvia Gunter and Arthur Burk, *Blessing your Spirit* (Birmingham, AL: The Father's Business, 2005), p. xi.
3 Brian D. McLaren, *Why Did Jesus, Moses, the Buddha and Mohammed Cross the Road?* (London: Hodder & Stoughton, 2012), p. 112.
4 John Trent and Gary Smalley, *The Blessing: Giving the Gift of Unconditional Love and Acceptance* (Nashville, TN: Nelson, 2011), p. 211.
5 Jack W. Hayford, *Blessing Your Children*, 2nd edn (Ventura, CA: Regal Books, 2012), p. 61.
6 Fruh, *Forgotten Blessing*, p. 130.
7 George Barna, *Transforming Children into Spiritual Champions* (Ventura, CA: Regal Books, 2003), pp. 77–9.
8 'A liturgy for receiving the father and mother blessings' is found in the Appendix at the end of this book.
9 Hayford, *Blessing Your Children*, p. 86.

8 Blessings in battle

1 Roy Gane, *Leviticus, Numbers*, NIV Application Commentary (Grand Rapids, MI: Zondervan, 2004), p. 703.
2 Gane, *Leviticus, Numbers*, p. 690.
3 I heartily recommend Gane's witty and lively *Leviticus, Numbers*, pp. 687–715.
4 John H. Walton, *Genesis*, NIV Application Commentary (Grand Rapids, MI: Zondervan, 2001), p. 100.
5 Gane, *Leviticus, Numbers*, p. 705.
6 Darrell L. Bock, *Luke*, IVP New Testament Commentary Series (Downers Grove, IL: IVP, 1994), pp. 122–4.
7 John Piper, 'What Does it Mean to Bless God?', Nov. 1978, <www.desiringgod.org/resource-library/articles/what-does-it-mean-to-bless-god>.
8 In the early 1970s Merlin Carothers wrote *Prison to Praise* (London: Hodder & Stoughton, 1972) and its sequel *Power in Praise* (Plainfield, NJ: Logos International, 1972), in which he maintained that we should praise God for all things in life and that if we did we would be delivered from the effects of all such problems. This reduces the place of praise

to a technique, and you may like to look at my Grove booklet *Failure* (Nottingham: Grove Books, 1987), pp. 10–11.

9 Blessing the land

1 *Common Worship: Daily Prayer*, Special Occasions, Rogation Days, p. 537.
2 F. David Peat, *Blackfoot Physics* (London: Fourth Estate, 1995).
3 Walter Brueggemann, *The Land* (London: SPCK, 1978), p. 52.
4 Russ Parker, *Failure* (Nottingham: Grove Books, 1987), p. 20.
5 Parker, *Failure*, p. 20.
6 Fred Bahnson and Norman Wirzba, *Making Peace with the Land* (Downers Grove, IL: IVP, 2012), pp. 12–20.
7 Russ Parker, *Healing Wounded History: Reconciling Peoples and Healing Places* (London: Darton, Longman & Todd, 2001; SPCK, 2012), pp. 16–38.
8 Jonathan Wilson-Hartgrove, *New Monasticism: What it has to Say to Today's Church* (Grand Rapids, MI: Brazos Press, 2008), p. 39.
9 Wilson-Hartgrove, *New Monasticism*, p. 39.
10 Bede, *The Ecclesiastical History of the English People* (London: Burns, Oates & Washbourne, 1935), pp. 161–5.
11 Wilson-Hartgrove, *New Monasticism*, p. 39.
12 Adam Nicolson, *Arcadia: The Dream of Perfection in Renaissance England* (London: Harper Perennial, 2009); quoted in 'Rogation Sunday: Worship Resources' on the Worcester Diocese website, <www.cofe-worcester.org.uk/pdf_lib/27.pdf>.
13 Roy Godwin and Dave Roberts, *The Grace Outpouring: Blessing Others Through Prayer* (Eastbourne: David C. Cook/Kingsway, 2008), p. 161.
14 Rebekah Brettle and Lyndall Bywater, *Neighbours, Transform Your Street! Bringing Prayer to our Neighbours, Bringing Community Back to our Streets* (Lancaster: Sovereign World, 2012).
15 Brettle and Bywater, *Neighbours, Transform Your Street!*, pp. 161–9.
16 A Blessing for a Town, in 'Prayer Blessings', <www.streetpastors.co.uk/Portals/0/Street Pastors/In Use/documents/ prayer/PrayingBlessings.pdf>, pp. 4–5.
17 Resources for holding street blessing and rogation services can be found at: *Celtic Daily Prayer: Inspirational Prayers and Readings from the Northumbria Community* (London: Collins, 2005); 'Blessing of the Land', pp. 200–2; 'Rogation Blessing', <www.letallcreationpraise.org/worship-services/rogation-blessing>; 'Rogation Sunday: Worship Resources', <www.cofe-worcester.org.uk/pdf_lib/27.pdf>; 'Rogation and Ascension', <www.fullhomelydivinity.org/articles/rogation and ascension.htm>.
18 Antony Billington, 'Blessing – Understanding it and Praying for it', <www.licc.org.uk/uploaded_media/1325590716-Blessing Essay.pdf>, p. 4.

10 Learning to pronounce blessings

1 Barbara Brown Taylor, *An Altar in the World* (Norwich: Canterbury Press, 2009); quoted in <www.oprah.com/spirit/An-Altar-in-the-World-Excerpt-Barbara-Brown-Taylor_1/4#ixzz2eTmmChjV>, p. 2.

2 Brown Taylor, *An Altar in the World*, pp. 3–4.

3 Brown Taylor, *An Altar in the World*, p. 4.

4 Daniel Fusco home blog <www.danielfusco.com/blog/pronouncing-blessing-a-lost-art/>.

5 Jack W. Hayford, *Blessing Your Children*, 2nd edn (Ventura, CA: Regal Books, 2012), p. 98.

6 This may be found in my *Healing Wounded History: The Workbook* (London: Darton, Longman & Todd, 2004).

7 An alternative might be to use the 'Prayer for Honouring Leaders' in my *Wild Spirit of the Living God: Prayer Poems for the Journey*, Acorn Christian Healing Foundation, Whitehill Chase, High Street, Bordon, Hants. GU35 0AP, or see <www.acornchristian.org>.

11 Blessing prayers for various occasions

1 From *Blessing Your Spirit* (2005), © Sylvia Gunter, The Father's Business, P.O. Box 380333, Birmingham, AL 35238, <www.thefathersbusiness.com>.

2 Sr Ruth Fox OSB, Sacred Heart Monastery, Richardton, North Dakota, 'A Non-traditional Blessing', 1985. Originally published in *Living Faith*, 1989. Used by permission of Sr Ruth Fox.

3 *Common Worship*, Principal Services, Holy Communion, Further Short Prefaces and Blessings – <www.churchofengland.org/prayer-worship/worship/texts/principal-services/holy-communion/furtherblessings.aspx>.

4 Worldwide Mission Fellowship – adapted from <www.wwmf.org/category/prayer-fuel/>.

5 The London Institute for Contemporary Christianity – see <www.licc.org.uk/prayerworks/prayer-journeys/how-to-pray-blessing/>. Words by Bev. Shepherd, LICC. www.licc.org.uk.

6 Rural Church Support Network for Yorkshire and The Humber, May 2006 – see <www.crc-online.org.uk/downloads/Rogation Material 2006.pdf>.

7 Rural Church Support Network for Yorkshire and The Humber, May 2006 – see <www.crc-online.org.uk/downloads/Rogation Material 2006.pdf>.

8 Faith and Worship website. Christian Prayers and Resources: Celtic Blessings from other Sources – see <www.faithandworship.com/Celtic_Blessings_and_Prayers.htm>.

9 The Northumbria Community, *Celtic Daily Prayer: Inspirational Prayers and Readings from the Northumbria Community* (London: HarperCollins, 2005), pp. 201–2. Used by kind permission of the publisher.

10 Adapted from Praesidium of Warriors of St Michael, Clergy Simple Blessing of a Home – see <www.pwsm-ri.org/Ritual-Prayers/Clergy-Simple-Blessing-Of-A-Home.html>.

11 Island Ireland website, Irish Blessings and Prayers – see <www.islandireland.com/Pages/folk/sets/bless.html>.

12 Russ Parker, 'Ending of Days', in *Wild Spirit of the Living God: Prayer Poems for the Journey*, Acorn Christian Healing Foundation, Whitehill Chase, High Street, Bordon, Hants. GU35 0AP, or see <www.acornchristian.org>.

13 See <http://tacomaweekly.tripod.com/Irish-Quotations.html>.

14 See <www.searchquotes.com/search/May_your_house_be_filled_with_laughter/>.

15 Island Ireland website, Irish Blessings and Prayers – see <www.islandireland.com/Pages/folk/sets/bless.html>.

16 Island Ireland website, Irish Blessings and Prayers – see <www.islandireland.com/Pages/folk/sets/bless.html>.

Appendix: A liturgy for receiving the father and mother blessings

1 This liturgy is from Christian Healing Ministries, Jacksonville, Florida. Used and adapted with permission.